how to start a home-based

Fashion Design Business

Angela Wolf

gpp®

Guilford, Connecticut

Copyright © 2012 by Morris Book Publishing, LLC

Interior spot art licensed by Dreamstime.com
Photos on pages 66 and 165 (left and right) courtesy of Gregg Rizzo
Photos on pages 155 and 165 (middle) courtesy of Johnson Rauhoff

Models: Amy McWhirter (page 155), Jen Ort (page 165, left), Trisha Bettich (page 165, middle), and Lanie VonBehren (page 165, right)

Editorial Director: Cynthia Hughes Cullen
Editor: Tracee Williams
Project Editor: Lauren Brancato
Text Design: Sheryl P. Kober
Layout: Sue Murray

Library of Congress Cataloging-in-Publication Data is available on file.

ISBN 978-0-7627-7877-5

Printed in the United States of America

10 9 8 7 6 5 4 3 2 1

This book is dedicated to my husband, Winn; my parents, Linda and Richard Boyer; and my grandparents, Gene and Shirley Stowell. Without your love, prayers, support, and encouragement I would have never made it this far in my career, and I can never thank you enough.

Contents

Acknowledgments

A special thank you to my husband, Winn, for all your love, support, patience, and encouragement. You have been there from the beginning of my fashion career, talking me into putting on my very first fashion show. You have been there for it all—from challenges to successes, what a ride it has been. Thanks for always believing in me, but mostly, thanks for being my best friend.

To my mother, Linda Boyer, for all your guidance, prayers, and support. Thanks for traveling to shows with me, never complaining when I would sneak fabric from your stash, allowing me to test patterns on you, my first sewing machine, and just being a great friend.

To my father, Richard Boyer, for instilling in me a solid confidence to believe anything is possible. You always encouraged me to strive for first and never settle for less.

Teresa and Julie, my sisters, for always stepping up to help me out, from ripping out seams to helping with my fashion shows. You both are the best!

To my grandparents Gene and Shirley Stowell for your love and support. Thanks for your many words of wisdom and encouragement and for being so special in my life. I feel so blessed.

Marge and Walt Wolf, thanks for your wisdom, guidance, strength and support.

A special thank you to my clients. There are so many of you that I could never start naming because I would be sure to leave someone out, and you know that would kill me. You all are the reason I was able to create a successful business and why I am able to write this book, and I thank you all from the bottom of my heart. Thank you for all the lessons, advice, memories, and friendships. Thank you!

To those that added to book: Janet Pray, president of the American Sewing Expo and Islander Sewing System. After I won the Passion for Fashion in 2008, Janet became a priceless mentor in my career and a great friend, I thank you so much for everything, and I look forward to new adventures with you. Marsha Brenner, executive director of the Apparel Industry Board Inc., is a great mentor to many fashion designers in the Chicago area and contributor to the fashion industry. Thanks for your guidance. Susan Glick, vice president, Women's Apparel Merchandise Mart Properties, is a well-respected expert in the fashion industry. Thanks for your encouragement. Joi Mahon, my fellow ASDP member, fashion designer and winner of the 2009 Passion for Fashion, thanks for your input. I always enjoy working with you and sharing a few laughs. Linda Stewart, fellow ASDP member, and alteration expert, thanks for sharing your story and encouraging others in the sewing industry through your writing and teaching.

Thanks to Tracee Williams and all those at Globe Pequot Press for this great opportunity and all your behind-the-scenes work.

To all my friends for standing by my side, their support and encouraging words, the occasional forced modeling in my fashion shows or behind-the-scenes delegator, you are all great, and I cherish your friendship.

Introduction

From a very young age I had a love for fashion and sewing. In high school I would sneak fabric from my mother's stash and try my hand at designing. Not understanding pattern directions, I would lie on the fabric and have my sisters sketch around me with chalk; it resembled a crime scene, as if we were tracing around dead bodies. I would cut out the fabric, use myself as a mannequin, and come up with some pretty cute, wearable styles. My creative passion never ceased from that point on, and it still continues today, although I'm happy to say my technique has come a long way.

I attended college to study business, but I would sew and design in my free time, never giving up on my fashion dreams. My graduation gift from my family—a new sewing machine and serger —started me off on my current path. I began studying pattern making, draping, and couture sewing. I would read and then practice, read, practice again, and on and on. After an initial push from my husband, I held an informal fashion show. I rented a small restaurant and invited all the ladies I knew (I am sure the free wine had something to do with the fabulous turnout) and showcased my designs. That show launched my custom apparel business.

Not having the connections or resources from attending a fashion-design college posed somewhat of a challenge. I wasn't sure what the "rules" were in the fashion industry, from getting an original garment into stores to designing a cohesive collection. I was insecure and very naive, but I did have a business background, and I loved designing clothes. I just made things work. This book is filled with some of the experiences I've had through the years, some good and some not so good. I want to share these with you to help you get started on the right track and hopefully avoid some of the pitfalls that soak up your time, money, and energy. When someone asked me what I was writing about, my reply was, "I am writing the book that I would have killed to have had access to when I started out," from information about the initial design stage to understanding how to price garments to running a fashion business out of your home. There are a lot of books available (I have included my favorites in the appendix) that can help the designer once they are ready to manufacture their apparel and sell to the larger retailers. But considering the statistics on the success of fashion designers, this can be a little daunting and downright scary. The information lacking in many of those books is how to start smaller without a large cash injection, which is where this book comes in. Regardless of whether you want to jump right in with both feet or just get your toes wet, this book can guide you through the entire process, from setting up with the correct licenses and business structure to laying out a plan for success. You will gain a quick overview of some of the legalities in the fashion industry along with resources and contacts that will work with new designers like yourself. I ran my business from home for many years, so I share with you how I made this work and what triggered me to draw the line and expand to a commercial studio.

One of the biggest challenges as a newly self-employed fashion designer, besides being cash poor, is acquiring the confidence to price your work appropriately. This is even more important when focusing on custom apparel. Why is it that we do not have a problem paying $150 for a plumber to stop by for an hour, but we find it hard to rationalize charging what we should for a custom couture gown? Always keep in mind, just because you work from home does not mean you need to discount your services. Even when I added alterations to the business I would charge based on a decent hourly rate. I recall a customer asking why I was so much more expensive than the dry cleaners. I asked her if the dry cleaners allowed her to try on her clothes so they can pin for a perfect fit. No. Enough said. I was not just selling a sewing job, I was selling a brand image. If you strive to be an expert in your field, you can quickly acquire a reputation that people won't mind paying extra for. Now this is related primarily to custom apparel, but take a closer look at some of the ready-to-wear collections. I can find jeans for $24 at Old Navy or $300 at Nordstrom. Why is that? Sure the fabric and construction play a major role, but the designer plays an even bigger role. That is branding at its finest. There is an entire chapter on marketing, public relations, and branding (chapter 10). Creating your own brand image from the beginning is important and allows your marketing efforts to be consistent.

With today's technology and social media craze, there are many opportunities as a fashion designer to get your name and brand out quickly. The chapter on creating social media buzz (chapter 9) walks you through setting up a strong presence on the Internet without spending a penny, from coming up with content that your audience wants to read to creating a strategic marketing campaign to surround your brand image. You might be starting out small, but you can market yourself just like the well-known designers. And don't worry if you are not computer savvy; the steps are very basic.

This book is filled with resources that you will be able to use for years to come. I have listed some of my favorite fabric suppliers that have lower minimums, books and magazines that can take you to the next level, tips on free downloads from some fantastic websites, and lots more. I hope you enjoy some of my real-life stories—remember to always keep a sense of humor. Even some of the worst mistakes can turn into great opportunities, like the story of my strange fitting jacket. I had just graduated from college, so my wardrobe left a little to be desired. My future husband called at around ten in the morning and invited me to a business event that night. He said he would pick me up at six o'clock and I should dress in a suit. I quickly pulled out fabric and sewed together an adorable pink and-grey plaid pencil skirt and tailored jacket. Finishing just fifteen minutes before he arrived, I tried on my new outfit. Very cute and fashionable, but something was weird. My shoulder felt tight, and the slender-cut two-piece sleeve was wrinkling at the elbow. Oh boy! I sewed the sleeves on backward, and of course my sleeves were very fitted. There was not time to fix this, and I really did not want to cancel, so I found that if I stood very straight with my shoulder slightly back and held my hands slightly behind my hips, the jacket looked great. I made it through the dinner, and later in the ladies' room, a woman commented that she just loved my suit. I was thrilled but had to hold in a burst of laughter when she added, "And I have never seen such perfect posture." I received so much business from that one event; what could have been a disaster turned into a profitable evening. Opportunities are everywhere, so let's get started!

When we think of fashion designers, our minds immediately think of the glamour. The runway show, gorgeous models, celebrity attention, the prestige. I call this the 1 percent glamour; the other 99 percent is hard work and dedication. As Princeton Review points out, only one fashion designer out of 160,000 will enjoy international fame. Although these statistics are true, if you have the talent, dedication, and drive, then nothing can stop you from attaining your dream as a fashion designer. So are you ready to take on the challenge? This chapter is designed to give you some insight into the life of a self-employed fashion designer.

Traits of a Fashion Designer

There are so many different avenues in the fashion realm you can tap into. The possibilities are endless. The best news is that you do not need a lot of money to start. Today's technology offers new opportunities for designers to enter the fashion industry in their own way. While the idea of becoming a fashion designer is very exciting and intriguing, you really need to ask yourself some serious questions and take into consideration the realities of this business. The fashion industry is one of the most competitive and cutthroat there is. Whether you choose to work for another designer or start on your own, as a fashion designer you are just one of many who can be "in" today and "out" tomorrow. But don't let that scare you away from reaching for your dreams; just know that you need to be thick-skinned, and never quit learning and evolving.

A fashion designer should have an eye for color and detail along with a sense of balance and proportion. Communication skills are vital in all aspects of the business, from working with contractors to selling your line to pleasing your clients. Although, there are successful fashion designers that cannot sew, sewing and pattern-making skills are an important aspect in understanding clothing construction. Not to mention being able to test your own patterns for fit and design issues can save you time and money.

Dedication and Commitment

A fashion designer who is also self-employed will wear a lot of hats. You need to be able to commit everything you have to offer—physically, mentally, and financially. High stress, long hours, and tight deadlines are part of everyday life. This is important to understand, because dedication and commitment are the only ways you will survive the schedule and work load. Ask any business owner, and they will tell you it can take years to get established and build a client base. Success rarely comes overnight. Before you jump in, there needs to be 100 percent commitment to your new adventure from you and anyone else who will be personally involved.

Creativity

I like this definition of creativity from Dictionary.com (based on the Random House Unabridged Dictionary):

> *CRE-a-TIV-i-ty noun*
> *1. The state or quality of being creative.*
> *2. The ability to transcend traditional ideas, rules, patterns, relationships, or the like, and to create meaningful new ideas, forms, methods, interpretations, etc.; originality, progressiveness, or imagination.*

As a fashion designer, creativity is one of the most important traits you must already have or eventually acquire. Creativity is what makes you stand out among the countless other fashion designers, and I am not only referring to the clothing. Maybe you design a simple, classic line of women's apparel, but it is your unique marketing strategy that could tip your brand over the edge above other less-innovative designers. Many artists will tell you they have a gift for creativity or they were born with it, but this is not to say you cannot acquire creativity through training, studies, and practice. Fashion magazines, sewing techniques, fabric manipulation, pattern draping, and sketching are only a few of the resources you have at your hands to advance your level of creativity. Go for it!

The True Reality

When you start you need to be realistic regarding the time and energy you can afford to throw into this business venture. As a full-time designer, twelve-hour days are a normal routine. But this is your business, and if that schedule does not work for your home life, you need to adapt the business plan accordingly. For example, if you decide to focus on designing custom apparel, you have the option of creating your own schedule by the jobs you choose to take on. On the other hand, if you plan on designing a collection to sell to stores, then you will most likely need to adhere to the general production schedule in order to fulfill your sales.

Being a fashion designer is much more than sketching beautiful dresses. In fact, you will be designing less than 10 percent of the time. Managing the entire process of a garment, from the first sketch to the final product, requires various skills, from style sense, knowledge of fabrics, estimating how much fabric to purchase, and marketing and sales. And don't leave out bookkeeping, which seems to be a dreaded task among us creative people. Organization will also be key to your sanity on a normal workday, while you are juggling the many responsibilities of a home-based business owner.

Fashion and Trends

As a fashion designer, keeping an eye on the emerging and existing fashions and trends is very important. I am not talking about copying designs from other fashion designers; I am simply talking about staying abreast of what is out there right now and what your potential competition is designing. That doesn't mean you have to follow the pack or alter your design aesthetic; just being aware can save you money and time. You can design the best maxi dress ever, but if the maxi dress went out of fashion last season, you will be left behind or shortening a line of dresses real fast. If you are in menswear, you will not want an entire collection of pleated pants when the flat front, straight leg is being shown in every fashion magazine. Get the idea?

Even if you decide to design custom, one-of-a-kind garments, keeping up on the trends is helpful to your clients. Many of my custom clients ask, "What skirt length is in right now?" or "How long are the jackets for fall?" Although I might have been designing an evening dress for that particular client, having the answer to her fashion-related questions or wardrobe dilemma was a way for me to showcase my expertise and knowledge. Little did I know, eventually I would even get paid for this advice by writing fashion columns and wardrobe styling.

Personality Check

Deciding which division of the fashion industry you decide to enter will also depend on your personality traits. Custom apparel, alterations, or any other field where you deal with clients one-on-one will require you to work with many diverse personalities. Polishing up on your people skills is a must if you work with clients. I remember when I first started doing alterations, many of my new clients would tell me how miserable the tailor in town was.

"He does great work, but he is always so ornery!" If you were that tailor, that is a bittersweet gossip chain. To have a reputation of being the best tailor in town, yet clients leave you because you are grumpy will put you in a prime position to lose business to a more-personable competitor.

If you decide to create a line and only sell to stores, you will still need to work with sales reps, store buyers, and contractors. A professional image is critical in order to open doors to your clothing line, just another reason to polish up on your business etiquette and communication skills.

Traits of an Entrepreneur

Creative
Inquisitive
Driven
Goal-oriented
Independent
Confident
Calculated-risk taker
Committed
Avid learner
Self-starter
Hard worker
Resilient
High energy level
Integrity
Problem-solving skills
Strong management and organizational skills

Isolation

If you work from home and do not have employees, this can make for a very lonely environment.

This is probably the hardest part for a self-employed fashion designer. Be careful that you do not become disassociated with society. Make sure you meet

Don't Give Up

Self-employment requires dedication and commitment. There are times when you might be ready to throw in the towel, but stay focused and don't give up. I recall an instance after being in business for a few years. I was twenty-six years old, working endless hours, day in and day out, by myself. My girlfriends called, wanting me to join them for a Saturday shopping day and then a night on the town. I looked at the stack of clothing that needed to be finished by Monday, and I knew there was no way I could give up those hours, so I begrudgingly passed on the invitation. At that time, I remember thinking I would do anything to have a "real job" just to be able to pick up a paycheck on Friday and not think about work until Monday! I look back now, and I am so glad I did not give up.

friends for lunch or go out to dinner—just get out of the house! I am laughing out loud while I write this, however, because I can count on two hands how many times I have taken the time to grab lunch with a friend in the last fifteen years. On the other hand, I do go out to dinner quite often. Even if it is just a coffee, get out there and mingle. Who knows—your next prospective client might be waiting for her latte in front of you.

Being Self-Employed

If you are only going into business for the prestige and vacation time, you might want to re-analyze your venture or at least buy a large quantity of lottery tickets. In all reality, self-employment is fundamentally about taking risks, and being self-employed requires a certain personality, a strong drive to succeed, and persistence. Entrepreneurs are described as innovative, disciplined, and calculated.

The US Small Business Administration statistics show that seven out of ten new businesses last at least two years. Only five out of ten—one-half—will make it past five years, only one-third make it to ten years, and only one-quarter make it over fifteen years. So what is it that the failed businesses are missing? After scanning numerous business articles, these seem to be the top four reasons for failure:

1. Starting a business for the wrong reason
2. Poor management
3. Lack of planning
4. No website

Those reasons are so basic, but they seem to be at the core of small business failure.

So do you think you have what it takes to become your own boss? Despite unknown challenges and obstacles that have passed through my life, the passion of designing beautiful clothes is what drives me to never give up. I hope in fifteen years you will be able to say the same.

Ask Yourself . . .

If you do an Internet search for "self-employment quiz," all kinds of questionnaires come up. After taking a handful of quizzes myself, I see a few common denominators. They all ask questions relating to risk management, long working hours, and motivation. These are serious personality traits to take into consideration before you try to

Self-Assessment Quiz

1. Do you need constant guidance and motivation? ❏ Yes ❏ No
2. Do you find it difficult to adapt to new circumstances? ❏ Yes ❏ No
3. Do you enjoy problem solving? ❏ Yes ❏ No
4. Do you finish what you start? ❏ Yes ❏ No
5. Would you consider yourself more of a leader than a follower? ❏ Yes ❏ No
6. Do you enjoy taking risks? ❏ Yes ❏ No

Someone with an entrepreneurial spirit would answer "yes" to questions 3 through 6 and "no" to 1 and 2. If you answered otherwise on any of the questions, those are the weaknesses that you will need to improve on. Just remember, going into business for yourself is a risk at any level, and you will need personal drive and a desire for success in order to make it to the top.

start your own business. This is not to say that if you are lacking in one these traits you cannot start a successful business. Simply being aware of where you might be lacking enables you to begin strengthening a potential weakness.

Job and Salary Stats in the Fashion Industry

Thanks to TV shows like *Project Runway* and *Fashion Star,* along with the media craze for fashion, many people are chasing the glamour by seeking careers in the fashion industry. Unfortunately, the stats show a bleaker side of the reality. According to the US Department of Labor Bureau, statistics show that the job availability for fashion designers is not going to increase more than 2 percent through the year 2018. That is not real promising, considering there are already fewer job openings than job seekers. With jobs in the fashion industry so difficult to come by, self-employment is a very viable option.

The starting salaries for a fashion designer tend to be very low. As a new designer, you will need to showcase your talents and skills before an employer will compensate accordingly. The median salary for a fashion designer in 2010 was $64,530, with an hourly rate of $31.02. On average the salaries ranged from $32,500 to $130,890. These are goods numbers to keep in mind as you formulate your business plan, especially when we talk about allotting for your time in order to accurately price your garments.

Second Job

The day we can work for ourselves and make a salary to support our lifestyle and our business is a great day. Until then, a second job is not a desire, just a necessity for survival. Starting my business right out of college, I was used to being broke. I bartended through college, so that was a natural for my second job. The positive: Bartenders are paid quite well, the tips are usually good, and your customer service skills will be tested to the limit. The negative: the late hours. I would see clients for custom clothing during the day, so the evening hours of my second job were a perfect marriage the first few years.

The passion for designing clothing will consume your entire life. Holding a second job in order to create your business becomes very hard to deal with—especially the long hours working both jobs. When I look back, I wish I would have taken a second job at Nordstrom, Neiman Marcus, or Barney's in order to learn and experience the retail side of what I was working so hard to create. What a valuable piece of information that would have been, to know firsthand what clients are looking for, their likes and dislikes, not to mention the wealth of information I would have acquired about fit.

The reality of the matter is that if you are going into business for yourself, unless you have financial support from somewhere else, you will need a second job in order to sustain a steady income. Choose your job wisely and make the best of your time.

Networking and Support

Word of mouth is going to be one of your best allies in creating a brand and an image for your clothing, which is why networking is vital in building a successful business. Networking also offers a support system of other business owners. Your location and budget will dictate where you network, but there are many options to choose from.

Family Support

Starting my business right out of college, my parents and grandparents were my biggest supporters. The gift of a sewing machine and serger was a priceless contribution in order for me to start my business. Since then, my husband has also been added to my support system. But it's not the monetary gifts that are important here, it's having the emotional support. As with any business, there are challenges and trials along with the small successes, and having support from close friends and family is priceless. I can recall a few times in my career that I was ready to throw in the towel, and it was my family that encouraged me to continue on.

If you have a spouse and children at home, it is critical you have their support and encouragement, especially if you are going to work from home. It is very difficult separating home life from your work when they are both in the same location.

Community Organizations

Another great way to get your name out and build your business is to join local organizations such as the following:

■ Rotary (www.rotary.org): An international organization with local clubs, members focus on getting involved in their communities on a volunteer basis, connecting with other professionals, and using skills to help people, among other things. This is a great networking organization.

■ Chamber of Commerce: A local organization that offers networking, training, and business development activities for entrepreneurs. Many benefits to small businesses and entrepreneurs include discounts on services such as health care. Oftentimes the chamber of commerce has special programs for new businesses on various topics, for example, training, education, funding, grant options, and mentoring.

■ Business Networking International (BNI; www.bni.com): Made up of professionals, this is a great support system not only locally but internationally. Most chapters offer weekly meetings, which is a great way to meet other professionals, not to mention that it gets you out of the house for an hour or two.

Find Others in Your Field

Thankfully technology has allowed us to connect with people all over the world with a click of a mouse. As a fashion designer there are many different components of our business: sewing, pattern making, fabric sourcing, not to mention simply running a business. There are numerous websites and organizations to meet people in your field. Here are a few to get you started, all of which I participate in and highly recommend:

- Fashion Group International Inc. (FGI; www.fgi.org): The mission of FGI is to help its members become more effective in their fashion careers. They offer insight to major trends and access to business professionals. This great organization offers online resources as well as local chapters in the larger cities. The events are a great way to network in the fashion industry.

- Association of Sewing and Design Professionals (ASDP; www.sewing professionals.org): This national organization's mission is to support individuals engaged in a sewing and design business, in both commercial and home settings. They offer a community of sewing professionals with a variety of expertise including custom apparel, formal and bridal, pattern making, tailoring and alterations, and fashion design. They offer local chapters in many cities and have an online community with members who are very helpful and generous with resources and information.

- Fashion Business International (FBI; www.fashionbizinc.org): Based in Los Angeles, California, this organization is a wealth of information. They offer seminars and networking opportunities if you live in the LA area; otherwise you can join their online classes. You can even take their online classes without being an official member.

- Apparel Industry Board Inc. (AIBI; www.aibi.com): AIBI offers nurturing and support to designers based in Greater Chicago. They also offer seminars related to the business side of fashion along with networking opportunities.

- LinkedIn (www.linkedin.com)—LinkedIn is a business-based website. This is a perfect place to connect with others professionals not only in your local community, but in your field worldwide. There are groups that you can join that offer a wealth of information such as the Custom Tailors and Designs Association. More to come on this in chapter 9.

Giving Back

There is truth in the belief that giving is more fulfilling than receiving. In an age where we can consume our daily life with work, taking an hour or two a month to volunteer is just an added bonus in creating a well-rounded person. The choices are unlimited as to where you could donate your time and skills.

There are even areas to help with your sewing skills. Members of the American Sewing Guild offer their sewing skills during prom season. Prom dresses are donated from local residents, and the guild members alter the dresses for girls that cannot otherwise afford it. Just another way to give back.

Get Motivated!

Now that you have somewhat of an overview of what it is going to be like working for yourself, make a short list of what is really inspiring you to start this business. Include in your list all of the positives you have to offer, including personality traits, business knowledge, and other ways you feel you will be an asset to your business. Keep this list and add to it as you learn and evolve. If the time should come that you feel discouraged about your business or rather insecure (and unless you are a superhero, this will happen), review this list. There are many books and resources available in reference to motivation, starting a new business, and entrepreneurship. A few business magazines I have enjoyed are *Entrepreneur* and *Inc.;* both offer insights, advice, and inspiration into owning your own business.

So what part of the fashion industry are you interested in? There are many options available from the behind-the-scenes pattern and sample makers to the forefront designer. The next chapter will take you through some of the main fashion design jobs.

There are a few different areas in the fashion industry that a designer might want to focus on. Here I have listed some of the main categories. Keep an open mind while previewing these areas of expertise; you might find the need to focus on more than one category in order to generate enough cash flow when starting your business.

Becoming a Fashion Designer

As a fashion designer there are many categories for you to consider. Are you going to design for men, women, or children? Will you focus your attention on apparel or accessories or both? You might choose to design in more than one category, but it is important to stay focused and true to your design esthetic. It is better to start small and give 100 percent to being the best in that specific area than to spread yourself so thin that you end up with multiple mediocre collections.

Creating Your Own Collection

The thrill of designing your own collection is invigorating and really the ultimate high for a fashion designer. Unfortunately, when you run your own business, designing will only make up 10 percent of your work requirements, so make sure you enjoy every minute of this part. There are some designers that either team up with a business partner or work another label, just so they can focus on designing and not have to deal with the business side. This makes me think of Valentino and his business partner, Giancarlo Giannetti. Valentino had full reign in designing from the fashion to the runway, and his partner controlled and ran the financial end. There is a documentary movie called *Valentino: The Last Emperor* that is well worth watching, not just for the fashion but to see how the two think so differently when it comes to the business side. They exhibit a true rendition of how the creative side competes with the rational financial side. How fantastic to have someone to deal with the business side! Unfortunately, starting out, most of us are on our own dealing with the entire business.

Before you go any further you need to decide who you will be designing for. Envision your ideal client, not only his or her clothing taste but also the client's lifestyle. How old is your target demographic? Do they work during the day or stay at home with children? Do they travel? Keep the list going; the better you know your client, the better focused your collections will be.

In general, you need to design a collection that is cohesive, all while keeping your ideal client in mind. There are many opinions as to how many styles should be in your line, yet as a small designer, twelve to fifteen styles per collection is ideal. While designing your collection, take into consideration how your pieces will look hanging in a store or on your rack at a trade show. Do the colors complement each other? Can you mix and match your styles? Are your pieces wearable? All of these thoughts must stay on the forefront while designing each collection. Next you need to decide what items you will include in your collection. I met one designer who only focuses on one item: jackets. Although, I must say she has a gorgeous line of jackets and she seems to be doing really well with her line, I personally have lines of jeans, knit tops, jackets, and a few dresses, and I mix and match my fabrics among all the styles. You

A Cohesive Collection

When I first started out, I created an eighteen-piece collection to showcase my work to potential custom clients. For many informal fashion shows over the years, I would find gorgeous pieces of fabric and design a garment based on that piece of fabric, never taking into consideration how that outfit might look next to another. While my focus was on one-of-a-kind garments, this plethora of fabrics, styles, and colors seemed to work—until a retail buyer wanted to look at my collection. I wish I could have taken a picture of her face when she saw my rainbow of apparel displayed on her rack. In an instant, my eyes were opened to the importance of a cohesive collection. As a fashion designer, humility checks can come often, but don't get discouraged. Instead take each one as a little learning lesson.

might only have a line of dresses or gowns, and that is also just fine. Determine your specialty and focus. For example the woman with the jacket line mentioned she eventually wanted to add pants to her collection, but she sees this happening at least two years down the line.

Fashion and Trends

As mentioned earlier, it is important to keep an eye on fashion and trends in your area of fashion. There are many resources to assist in keeping you abreast of what is going on in the fashion world. *Women's Wear Daily,* Style.com, and ApparelNews.net are filled with invaluable information, including runway shows and trend forecasting. Keeping tabs on the upcoming trends does not mean you have to follow the trends; it is simply a good idea to know what people are wearing today and what will be coming out next season. Even if your designs are a more classic style, basic knowledge of the popular colors and skirt lengths for the following season can be very helpful in creating a collection that stores will want to carry.

But it is really important for you to stick within your own design aesthetic and not jump to follow every passing trend, because many of them are just that—passing.

It seems that the media's infatuation with celebrities is adding another twist to the fashion spectrum. From editorials to pictures that grace the covers of our magazines, the media plays a huge role in today's fashion. Not only do they help translate the current trends for the general public, they can create a lot of buzz about the designers themselves. Just look at what the media did for Jason Wu after he designed a gown for Michelle Obama.

The Schedule in the Fashion Design World

When designing a collection, you are always designing a year in advance. The women's ready-to-wear (RTW) and children's wear New York City markets are as follows for each fashion season:

Summer: October

Fall I: January

Fall II: February

Holiday and Resort: June

Spring: August

California Apparel News has compiled an international fashion calendar that you can download from their website (www.apparelnews.net). The calendar lists trade shows, textile shows, and fashion weeks along with links in order to find additional information and sign up for each show.

The Traditional Schedule

If you plan on selling your line at a trade show or holding a runway show during fashion week, you need to adapt your schedule to the market week and trade-show calendar. Keeping up with the production calendar can be a bit unnerving, but organization will help in this department.

On page 16 you can find an example of a production schedule larger companies follow.

Adapting Your Schedule on a Smaller Scale

When you are first starting out there is no reason to make yourself crazy designing so many different collections every year. Many designers only create two collections annually, focusing on Fall/Winter and Spring/Summer. Also keep in mind, as a smaller designer you have more flexibility for fast turnarounds. You might be able to offer twelve delivery dates a year within those two main collections. Some boutiques like this because they are not required to order such large quantities at first, especially when buying from a new designer.

Production Schedule

Month	Spring/Summer 2013	Fall/Winter 2013
March 2012	Research fabric and begin designing	
April 2012	Select and order fabrics	
May 2012	Create patterns Begin sampling	
June 2012	Collections developed	
July 2012	Create a production plan Finish sampling	
August 2012	Begin sales	
September 2012	Collections shown and sales continue	Research fabric and begin designing
October 2012	Sales finalized	Select and order fabrics
November 2012	Production materials ordered Production begins	Create patterns Begin sampling
December 2012	Supervise production	Collection developed
January 2013	Supervise production	Create a production plan Finish sampling
February 2013	Collection is completed Deliver to stores Collect payment	Begin Sales
March 2013	Continue deliveries Collect payment	Collections shown and sales continue
April 2013		Orders finalized
May 2013		Production materials ordered Production begins
June 2013		Supervise production
July 2013		Supervise production
August 2013		Collection is completed Deliver to stores Collect payment
September 2013		

Custom Apparel

Many fashion designers who know how to sew focus their efforts on the custom side of apparel; this is actually how I started my business. Most of the custom-apparel business comes from either the client's desire for something spectacular for an upcoming event or the need for something that fits. Starting out by designing custom apparel is a great way to get your name out there as a designer, and maybe this is where you will focus your business. There is a very viable market for custom apparel, not to mention creating gorgeous garments for your custom client can also draw attention to your RTW line, if you have one.

Designing apparel for select clients is very different than designing a ready-to-wear collection. In some ways your design freedom is limited because you need to design what that particular client is envisioning, all while keeping in mind their over-all body shape and personal styling needs. On the positive side, you can charge quite a bit more for custom work, thus allowing you to take advantage of nicer fabrics and utilizing intricate design or sewing techniques that you might not otherwise have a budget for with your RTW line.

Some of the technical skills required for custom apparel are sewing, pattern making, and the ability to fit a variety of shapes and sizes. Just as paramount are your communication skills, as you will be working with a particular client for weeks on end. Think of custom apparel as a six-week spa for your client, which is the average time to complete a custom garment. The client is there to feel special; she wants to be catered to and plans on leaving there with a fabulous outfit.

Original One-of-a-Kind Design

There are many factors that go into designing a custom garment. As the designer, your client is relying on your expertise, your fashion sense, and ultimately your advice. Probably one of the most challenging aspects of custom apparel is knowing when to say no. For example, if a client brings you a picture of a style she would like you to make, yet you know from experience the silhouette she has chosen will not flatter her body shape, it is your job to show her alternate styles that would be more flattering. This also holds true if your client desires a certain color that does not complement her skin tone, or a fabric that you know will not work with the particular design. Your client might not like hearing your suggestions, but ultimately you are the professional, and you are the one with the reputation to uphold. Gut instinct also plays a large role when deciding which custom clients to accept. Here is a little fact about gossip: If you make a client look fabulous, she will tell a handful of friends; if you screw up and your client is dissatisfied, she will tell everyone!

Many times clients think that since you can sew you will do anything, including knocking off a couture designer's look for a fraction of the price. Or the client simply wants a dress just like in a magazine but cannot locate her size. If you choose to take on jobs like this, at least make some changes from the designer's original work. There are legalities involved if you plan on copying another designer's work, and this is covered in more length in chapter 8.

Designing a Custom Garment

Here are some factors to take into consideration:

- The event or occasion—for example, dressy, casual, black tie
- Client's age
- Client's personal style
- Client's overall body shape
- Client's skin tone and hair color
- Client's overall request

Keeping Up to Date

When it comes to mastering sewing and fitting skills, there are many books, magazines, online classes, and tutorials available. Take advantage of many of the free tutorials on YouTube and select blogging sites. Sewing expos are another way to get hands-on training. One of my favorites is the American Sewing Expo (www.american sewingexpo.com) in Novi, Michigan. This expo offers many classes taught by talented instructors from all over the country.

The Association of Sewing and Design Professionals (ASDP) (www.paccprofessionals .org) holds an annual conference with first-class instructors and speakers. They also

Advancing Your Sewing Education

Here are a few resources to check out if you are interested in advancing your sewing education without going back to school:

- *Threads* magazine's *Fitting* DVD series
- PatternReview.com's online classes (www.patternreview.com)
- *SewStylish* magazine
- *Threads* magazine
- YouTube videos
- ASDP annual conference (www.paccprofessionals.org)
- American Sewing Expo in Novi, Michigan (www.americansewingexpo.com)
- American Sewing Guild (www.asg.org)
- *Islander Sewing Systems*
- PBS series *It's Sew Easy* (www.itssoweasytv.com)
- Sew and Stitchery Expo in Puyallup, Washington
- *Vogue & Butterick Designer Sewing Techniques* guidebook
- *Vogue Sewing* guidebook
- Craftsy.com

offer a certification program that will allow you to test your skill level in all aspect of a custom apparel business.

Finding Clients

Word of mouth is a priceless advertisement. If you design a custom garment for someone and they are satisfied, it is amazing how fast word travels. Most of my clients were referred from previous clients.

Holding an informal fashion show is a great way to show your talent to potential new clients. Invite your clients and then allow them to bring a guest. The fashion show can be made up of all new creations you have designed, or ask some of your previous clients to model their pieces. Clients love that; in fact, I have never had a client turn down an opportunity to show off their garment.

Social media marketing is a fast, easy, and inexpensive way to get your name out there from posting pictures of your work on Facebook to blogging about a new fabric you are working with. Chapter 9 will walk you through creating an entire social marketing campaign.

Client's Expectations

It is important to explain to your client everything they should expect in regards to their new custom garment before you even purchase the fabric. This can really save you both a headache later on. If the dress is going to take six weeks and five fittings, they need to know this up front. Regardless of how long the garment will take, give the client an experience to remember. When they arrive for their fittings offer them tea or coffee; make sure they are comfortable and at ease.

What is your client's expectation as to the quality you will deliver? Quality really depends on the price point of your garment, but typically the expectation with custom apparel is that the client is looking for exquisite quality. This not only includes the sewing, but the materials you choose for the garment. You could make two pair of pants, one out of an inexpensive polyester and one out of an Italian wool. Using the same pattern would mean the same amount of time would go into both pants, but they would look like night and day hanging next to each other. Keep this in mind when clients bring you their own fabric. You might not be able to (or want to) work with what they give you. The client might just like the color without understanding the quality or the characteristics of fabric, but you do. Why spend twenty hours designing a jacket out of an inexpensive fabric when the same job could create astounding results out of a finer fabric?

Contracts and Changes

Have the client sign a contract and place a 50 percent nonrefundable deposit down. This is a custom garment and if they change their mind, the odds that you will be able to sell the finished product to someone else are pretty slim. A contract not only gives you a professional image but will guarantee the client will have no doubts as to what to expect. In the contract you can state the timeline for the garment, what is expected from the client as far as what undergarments to bring to the fittings, and details of the garment to be made.

This is also a perfect opportunity to let them know your policies as far as any changes they make during the designing process; at what point do you charge more? I once had a client come in for her last fitting and decide she wanted a new collar on a blouse. This meant I had to rip out the entire collar, sew up a new one, and restructure the front of the blouse neckline. This ended up taking me longer to do than making the entire blouse, not to mention the extra fabric. Because I had given her a

Body Shapers

I recall when slimming body shapers came into being. This skintight, body-hugging garment magically transforms women's shapes; in fact they can lose inches of body mass. This story is about a mother of the bride who I designed a princess-seamed dress and tailored jacket for. The style was extremely fitted and included hours of tailoring and hand-beaded trim. The client arrived for her final fitting, tried on the finished garment, and guess what—she had been introduced to the product the day before and had miraculously lost a little over three inches around the waist and hip area! I will not even go into what the new bra did to her overall figure! After a body transformation like that, there was no way of getting my client back into her original undergarments. This is the exact reason you need to explain to your client, from the beginning, that they need to bring the exact undergarments and shoes they plan on wearing to every fitting. If anything changes there will be additional fees added to the price of the garment.

quote, I felt that I couldn't charge more for these changes. My husband proposed a great question. "When someone changes their mind in the middle of building a house, the additional fees are tremendous. What makes custom clothing any different?" From that point forward I initiated a formal contract for the clients to sign with the details of extra charges that they could incur. This list eventually included extra charges for excessive weight gain or loss (which really comes into play when working with brides), missed appointments, or changing undergarments after the final muslin fitting.

Weddings

Designing a wedding gown can be glamorous and exciting. The bride has a dream and you are fulfilling her dream with your talents. Sounds like a fairy tale to me, but usually weddings do not progress quite so smoothly. It is only fair to inform you what to prepare for and what to expect when working with a bride. From the personalities to the deadlines, I quickly came to the realization that an entire wedding can be put into four major categories:

1. The bride
2. The bridesmaids
3. The mother of the bride
4. The mother of the groom

Each category has its own rules. It is wise to analyze each of these elements and decide which one, if any, you will design for.

Definitely have a contract stating your policies, including your fee for missed appointments. Require at least a 50 percent nonrefundable deposit to start, and the remainder is due with the completion of the muslin fitting. Lastly, require the client to try on the finished gown and sign off as to their acceptance of the fit and style. If that sounds harsh, take a peek at David's Bridal policies: Absolutely no returns to the store, the dress must be paid in full before they will order it, and all alterations must be paid for in advance. There is a legitimate reason for these policies.

The Bride

Designing a wedding gown is very special, as you are going to be playing a major role in one of the most important days of a woman's life. From her initial dream dress to the hours leading up to the "I dos," designing a custom gown for a bride involves

> ### Designing a Bridal Gown
>
> Here are a few questions to consider:
>
> - Can the dress be made, and do you have the skills to complete it?
>
> - Will the dress flatter the bride?
>
> - Is there anything about the dress design that will not work?
>
> - Can you create this gown within the bride's budget?

much more than just a dress. The excitement and stress can affect personalities from fitting to fitting, not to mention drastic weight loss. Many times you will become the confidant and sounding board for the bride. It is important that you are a positive influence in the bride's entire experience.

A bride usually has an idea in mind about what she would like in a dress. Start by sketching out her vision and then take a good look at the overall design. This is where you need to be totally honest with your client and yourself. If something will not work, it is good to know right away. For example, a young girl brought me a sketch of a strapless gown. The front had a very low-cut V, and the back was cut clear down to the waist. She wanted the dress out of four-ply silk with no boning. There was no way this dress could stay up on the body without straps. The bottom line was that the engineering for that design would not work.

The Indecisive Bride

If a bride seems uncertain on what style or design she really wants, I would suggest sending her shopping. I am not saying you want to lose the client. You just want her to go try on wedding dresses so she can get a feel of the difference of each style and form an opinion of what looks the best on her. In fact, if you have the time, offer to be her consultant and take her shopping for an hourly fee. In reality, if the bride has not tried on gowns, she only knows what looks good on paper and not what looks and feels good on her. I have heard horror stories of brides wanting the full Cinderella gown, yet when the gown is completed, they hate it; it's too heavy or too full. Through time you will get a feel for each client's needs.

Scheduling

Once you have finalized a design for the bride, you will need to have a pretty austere schedule for fittings and the final garment completion date. Just be forewarned, the week before the wedding is absolutely crazy! Make a strong effort to have the bride's gown finished and out the door before that week arrives. The bride is dealing with a lot of stress and anxiety with her upcoming event; dress alterations at the last minute only add fuel to that fire.

The Bridal Party

Brides absolutely love the idea of having their bridesmaids in custom dresses. Many times the bride has designed the dress and chosen the fabric. The bridesmaids, on the other hand, are not always as thrilled about the custom gown idea when they see the price tag and time required for fittings. The other difficulty is that many times the bridesmaids live all over the country.

With the bridal party it is imperative to have a contract similar to the one for custom apparel. Be very clear on the number of fittings you foresee and what the extra charge will be for missed appointments. Require full payment and a signed contract by each bridesmaid before you order the fabric, just in case the decision is made to cancel the order.

Too Expensive

If it is apparent that the price of the custom dresses is not pleasing to the bridesmaids, do not lower your price to accommodate. Instead, offer suggestions like restyling, changing the hemlines, or adding embellishment to dresses they purchase at a retail store. This will not require as much time for each girl, the cost will be less prohibitive, and you still gain the business.

Overcoming Location Boundries

So what happens if the bridesmaids are thrilled to have custom dresses made and you find they live all over the country? Well there will obviously be difficulties having them stop by for fittings. Technology offers a unique fitting experience with a software program called Skype (www.skype.com). Skype is free; you both just need an account and a computer with a camera. You can easily walk them through taking their measurements. Shortly after, ship their muslin to them and see firsthand how the dress looks. The client just stands in front of their computer and you take notes as to fitting issues or pattern changes. You might even instruct them how to pin up a hem or mark a waistline.

If you choose to design dresses without seeing the client in person, make sure you are paid in full up front, including shipping costs. When shipping back and forth, make sure both of you ship with insurance and require a signature for delivery confirmation. This protects you as much as it protects your client.

Mother of the Bride

Mother of the bride gowns are some of my favorites to design. These women want to look beautiful, yet not outshine their daughters. They usually love the experience of a custom garment and will be your best walking advertisement for future business. With all the stress of wedding planning, this is a special way the mother can pamper herself.

Mother of the Groom

The mother of the groom is usually a little more behind the scenes for the entire wedding. The mother of the bride usually chooses her colors first, so the mother of the groom is left waiting. The mother of the bride is really involved with all the planning, whereas the mother of the groom is expected to go with the flow. I have found the mothers of the groom, in general, really enjoy the attention and experience of having a custom garment made. These women will also become your biggest fan if you make them look fabulous. Give her something to brag about.

Pricing

Probably the most challenging part of designing custom apparel is pricing your work. When you first get started, it will be a little challenging to predict the hours that will go into each garment, but through time you will get a handle on this. Consider taking a stroll through higher-end boutiques or department stores in your area and really pay attention to the quality and prices of clothing similar to what you are designing. Get an idea on overall pricing. Remember, you are offering your client a custom-made garment that fits them perfectly.

Fill in an estimated cost sheet with details on fabric, notions, labor, and anything else pertinent to the construction of the garment. Pretty basic. In chapter 6, see the "Estimated Cost Worksheet" on page 108 to get you started. The figures listed allow you to analyze the labor and materials closely, giving you a better chance at accurately assessing what a garment is going to cost you to make. You do not usually show this cost sheet to your client, in fact I usually keep this for my records only. But at least this allows you to give your client an estimate with a fairly accurate price range, like $1,200 to $1,500. Leave a little wiggle room in case you gravely underestimated the labor hours, especially when you first get started. On the other hand, if the garment comes in on the low side, the client will be thrilled.

Compare Quality and Pricing

Designing separates has always been my specialty. When I first started out, I really had a hard time pricing my work. For one thing, since I taught myself how to design and sew, my self-esteem was a little low. When learning on your own, you do not have the affirmations of a boss or superior. Another factor was the price of my wardrobe; it was made up of colored jeans from Express and tops I sewed myself. Until I started to personal shop for some of my clients, I had no idea women would pay $600 for a pair of ready-to-wear pants. While shopping at these higher-end department stores, I was able to compare the quality of my work with other designer labels. Taking the quality, the fabrics, and the styles into account, I realized I was way undercharging for my services. No wonder I was burning out! This was a great learning lesson.

Alterations

The alterations business is a very viable source of income. For those already working with clients in custom apparel and looking for an additional income, alterations can add a steady cash flow to your overall bottom line. Many of your current clients will appreciate the extra service, and you will be amazed how much you will learn about fit and clothing construction. At the same time, offering alterations can introduce your design work to potential clients.

I really wasn't interested in alterations at all, but it was owing to the persistence of my custom clients that I decided to give it a go. At first I dreaded the idea; I would rather make a garment from scratch any day over ripping one apart. But through time I realized that doing alterations was more than extra money, it was a great education. If you are fortunate enough to alter any higher-end apparel, pay attention to what is inside the garments. I realized that every time I ripped apart an Armani jacket or raised the sleeves on an Escada suit, it was like visiting the workroom of each designer—some impressive and some shockingly not! Not only was I able to improve my construction techniques by doing these alterations, I was able to master the art of fitting. Once you see the challenges many have when purchasing ready-to-wear garments, you might see great opportunities in the custom apparel and alteration business.

Time Management

I eventually came to enjoy the fast turnaround time of each project, and visiting with clients was a pleasure, but as months went by I realized I was spending all my time doing alterations and my fashion design career had been on hold. Be careful to manage your time wisely if you are only adding alterations as a side income.

The Business of Alterations

Whether you decide to do alterations as a full-time career or for a part-time cash flow resource, the business is the same. You will need to ask yourself what you know how to alter, what you would like to alter, and what you want to stay away from altering.

When deciding your alteration specialties, think of a doctor. If you have a broken foot, you are not going to go to the dermatologist. This is exactly the same in the alteration categories. Just because you are the best at a silk chiffon hem doesn't mean that you can sew lawn-chair cushions. This is very important because as soon as the word gets out that you sew, you will not believe what people will bring you to fix.

Every category mentioned requires different skills and some even require special equipment and a particular workroom layout. Even if you open a shop to run your

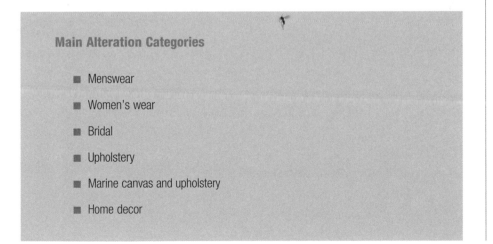

Main Alteration Categories

- Menswear
- Women's wear
- Bridal
- Upholstery
- Marine canvas and upholstery
- Home decor

> **True Story**
>
> I chose to only alter women's apparel. Unfortunately I had a hard time saying
> no at first. A call came from a client wanting to show off some new fabric her
> sister ordered from Italy. I barely got through the door and the sister handed over
> yards of thick, flowered upholstery fabric and asked to have her daughter's chair
> and lampshade covered, along with four pillows made for the bed. I immediately
> thanked her for thinking of me, but explained that I only work with women's
> apparel. The client adds, "Oh, Angela, you have made such beautiful things for
> me. You can sew anything, I am sure this won't take you long at all." I thought to
> myself, she's right, this won't take long, but a lampshade? So I declined again,
> with no success. The sister came back, pleading, "Please, I only trust you with
> this special fabric."
>
> Against my better judgment, I took the fabric. I covered the chair and made
> the pillows. The problem: I had never covered a lampshade (nor will I ever again).
> I spent days looking for information on how to cover the lampshade (this was
> pre-YouTube and Amazon days). I finally called the client and explained that
> everything was done except the lampshade and that I hadn't a clue how to do
> that. She came back with "Just cover it! Make it look good on the outside. I don't
> care what it looks like on the inside." So I did. Glue gun and all, three days of
> time, and a massive headache. Outcome: The lampshade turned out awful, and I
> lost both clients.

alteration business, it would be wise to keep true to what you are good at. Living on
Lake Michigan, I received many calls to fix torn boat canvas; thankfully there is a canvas repair shop just down the street that I could send people to. Guess what? They are
a "canvas repair shop." Would you bring them a wedding dress to alter?

Staying Current

There are books, videos, and blogs out there that will not only teach you to sew alterations, but even solutions to common fitting problems. It is important to understand
garment construction in order to help a client with fitting issues. If you can't compre-
hend how the garment is structured, how are you going to fix the problem? The best

way to attain this knowledge is experience. Practice on friends and family, practice on yourself, and practice sewing. For guidance you can turn to these resources:

- *Threads* magazine's DVD series *Fitting* (www.threadsmagazine.com)
- *SewStylish* and *Threads* magazines for fitting and sewing techniques (www.threadsmagazine.com)
- Fabric stores and some of the larger stores that offer classes
- PatternReview's online classes taught by experts in the sewing and fashion fields (www.patternreview.com)
- *Alterations for Professionals* (book on CD) by Linda Stewart (www.linda stewartcouturedesigns.com)
- The Association of Sewing and Design Professionals' online discussion list for fitting, sewing, and design issues (www.sewingprofessionals.org)
- Islander Sewing Systems (www.islandersewing.com)

Network and build relationships with other alteration specialists in your area. I am not saying all of them, just a few who you can relate to and are able to talk the same language with. If I go home and tell my husband about the difficulty I had fitting someone with a curved back, he is going to go into "trance mode." If you talk about the same issue to someone in your field, not only can they relate but they might have some good advice. These relationships are a definite benefit and a great way to share business while at the same time helping you to build a reputation. If someone brought me something to alter and I was not sure how to solve their problem or I was

Working Together

A friend of mine had been doing alterations for over fifteen years when her spouse became ill. She chose to send all of her clients my way; in return I promised to let them all know if she ever got into the business again. This was invaluable for increasing my client base, and many of these women became my custom-apparel clients. About seven years later, my friend's spouse passed away, and she decided to get back into the alteration business. By that time, I had built my custom-apparel business, and I was more than happy to refer clients back to her. We are still friends to this day and continue to refer clients back and forth.

too overloaded with my custom apparel work, I would refer the client to one of these sewing friends. The clients usually appreciated that I had a reliable place for them to go, and I knew they would receive the same quality service that I give. Am I giving my clients to the competition? No, I am simply networking and creating a base, not to mention—you never know where these relationships will go.

Finding Clients

The best way to find clients is word of mouth. If your work is praised by one client, she will tell friends, and those friends will tell their friends, and on and on. There's more on this in chapter 10, but here are a few ideas to get you started attracting new clients:

- Stop by local clothing stores, introduce yourself, and leave a business card.
- Dry cleaners are always looking for alteration experts.
- Create a Facebook page.
- Advertise in a church bulletin.
- Donate a gift certificate to a local charity auction.

Delivery versus Clients in Your Home

Where you reside and your current living conditions will determine how you choose to see clients. When I first started my business, I lived on the third floor of an apartment building—without an elevator. Needless to say, I picked up and delivered for the first few years. There are positives and negatives of both, but sometimes you might not have a choice.

Basic Home Pickup Checklist

Use the following checklist to determine if you should have clients come to your home:

■ Would you be in violation of any zoning laws?	❑ Yes ❑ No
■ Is your home easy to find and accessible?	❑ Yes ❑ No
■ Do you keep your house clean?	❑ Yes ❑ No
■ Is there a proper fitting area?	❑ Yes ❑ No
■ Does your family mind interruptions?	❑ Yes ❑ No

The benefit of visiting clients in their own home is that you never have to worry about clients stopping by unexpectedly. If you did not have time to clean the house or you detest shoveling the driveway, it will not matter one bit. The biggest drawback is the time and expense involved with traveling, not to mention the extra time spent in a client's home. This is something to consider when pricing your work. Think about adding a delivery surcharge to cover your gas and some of the travel time. Have you ever noticed the delivery surcharge when you order pizza for delivery? Even my lawn service has a gas surcharge. They are not doing this without reason, so take hints from these other service-oriented businesses.

Clients in Your Home

When allowing clients to visit your home, you might consider the policy of "by appointment only" so you are not faced with people stopping by at all hours. This is strictly for your family's sanity (and yours).

True Story

Be Safe—Trust Your Instincts!

I received a call from a potential new client needing alterations. She was supposedly referred by another client of mine. After missing her driveway three times, I found a narrow dirt path going back into the woods. The house was located near the beach, and the neighborhood was pretty nice overall, so I did not think anything of this backwoods location. I pulled up to a small house and was greeted by her husband. I follow him into their kitchen area, which was dark, dirty, and very messy—just a bit unnerving. I asked for his wife, and he claimed she would be right down. I waited for about ten minutes while he continued to talk about all sorts of weird things, but I saw no evidence of a wife anywhere. Then he said, "You know, while we are waiting for my wife, I need some alterations as well. Why don't you follow me to the basement and we'll get my things out of the way first." Yikes! I politely explained that I only alter women's apparel and that I was now late for my next appointment. I could not get back to my car fast enough! By the way, I never did see or hear from his wife again.

In order to prepare for clients to visit your home, you need to have certain standards in place. Cleanliness and organization are a must! Make sure you have a proper fitting area, good lighting, and a mirror to mention a few of the basics. Setting up your home for clients will be covered in the next chapter, but first and foremost you will need to check the zoning laws in your area to make sure you are legally allowed to have clients visit your home. If the zoning laws are not in your favor, you can always approach the local zoning board for an exception.

Policies

Having policies in place from the beginning will allow you more control over your business. Decide what your turnaround time will be; this will allow clients to know what to expect. Missed appointments are another common factor with alterations. What about a tardy client? Will you charge extra or even see them if they are over fifteen minutes late? I had this happen once. My schedule was completely full, and I usually allotted thirty minutes per alteration client. If one of my clients showed up twenty-five minutes late, clearly this would inflict on the time for my next client and continue to delay the schedule for the remainder of the day. As much as I hated to do this, I had to reschedule the client that was tardy for another day. She was less than thrilled, but she understood. The funny thing is the client was never late again.

Additional Policies to Consider

- **Clothing dropped off must be clean.** Cleaning clothing before they drop it off is a must. I can tell you horror stories of white garments with tanning cream residual and on and on. More importantly, if you alter a dirty garment and you press a stain, and the stain becomes permanent, who is responsible?
- **Fifty percent deposit.** I never require a deposit for alterations because my clients are all word of mouth. In over ten years of alterations, I was only stuck with a handful of items.
- **Clothing not picked up in sixty days will be donated to charity.** I did notice that the younger clients seem to have the biggest issue with picking up their garment within a certain time period. Maybe they found a different dress to wear or lost the desire for the item they were so excited to have altered. Because of the policy in place, I would call them and politely explain that if they did not pick up their garment before such and such date, I would be

donating it to Goodwill or some other organization. This usually brought the client in immediately, and they paid for their alteration. Even if they later donated their garment, at least I received my money.

Scheduling

It just makes business sense to create specific hours that you will see clients. Even if you require clients to have an appointment to visit, stick to the hours you have laid out for yourself. This will allow you scheduled time for clients and other scheduled time to sew.

For example, you can decide that you will only schedule clients from 10 a.m. to 6 p.m. Tuesday through Friday. With this schedule you know you can sew on Monday, on the weekend, and during the early morning hours without any interruptions.

Schedule Family Time

If you have a family, be careful to separate your business from the daily family life. More importantly, make time for your family even if you have to schedule it. This might sound crazy, but if you do not keep special times for your family, before you know it, the business will take over every hour of your entire life.

True Story

When I moved to a street-level condo, I began allowing clients to come to my home. Most clients would adhere to their appointment schedule, but there are always those few that just did not understand. I remember once getting out of the shower and hearing the doorbell ring; it was a client stopping by because she happened to be in the area—very awkward! Another time, I had my sisters in town for a weekend and another client stopped by with a pile of alterations. Instead of asking her to come back at a later time, I allowed her to proceed, and my beach day with my sisters turned into another work day. Being young and energetic, I allowed these unexpected interruptions, but it did not take long for my personal and business lives to become so intertwined that I began to lose my personal life. Try not to allow this to happen.

Pricing

Alteration pricing is pretty standard; just make sure you are paid for your time. Take into consideration your location, but just because you live in a small town does not mean you have to cut your prices. Check with the local dry cleaners for a price list and charge more than they do. With a dry cleaner, people just drop off their alterations already marked. In your business, you have to allot for the time to fit each client individually, especially if you are giving your expert advice.

For an extended price list, simply do an Internet search for "alteration price list," and you will have pages to scan through. Another source is JSM Tailoring Tools (www.jsmtailoringtools.com), which offers a computer program called *Pricing Alterations Made Easier* that covers the pricing of over six hundred alterations. Many alterations experts rely on and recommend this program.

I have been in alteration shops that post their current price list. I would not suggest doing this, only because there are times when a basic alteration can turn into a major alteration and you do not want to be tied to a generic price. Instead, I would mention the approximate cost to the client, especially if it was going to be an expensive alteration. If the alteration is going to cost them eighty dollars, let them know before you begin the work and allow them to agree or disagree. There are times a client might think an alteration is too expensive to salvage the particular garment they brought to you. That is okay, but it is better that they know up front. Clients do not like surprises!

When to Say No

As I mentioned earlier, it is important to know what you are capable of altering and ultimately what you prefer to alter. This will prevent hours of struggling over a project that you cannot figure out how to fix. I used to receive numerous requests to mend comforter covers, bed skirts, and pillowcases. I would explain that I only alter women's clothing. Be prepared: There are always the few who insist that since you sew you should be able to help them out anyway. Simply put, just say no and stick to what you are good at.

Costume Design

A costume designer is hired by a theater, dance, or opera company to design costumes for a film or stage production. A costume designer must be able to sketch, create patterns, drape, and sew. If you are interested in costume design you should approach your local art center or college and see what they have available. Often they are looking for additional talent to help or they will keep your name on file. It might not pay real well at first, but once you get your foot in the door there is potential if you do a good job. Here are a few avenues you can pursue if you are interested in costume design:

- Freelance designer—hired for specific production; can work on multiple productions at once
- Residential designer—hired for a series of productions; works on location
- Academic designer—usually an instructor or professor at a college

Costume designers can easily start by sewing and designing from home. When you venture into residential designing and teaching, you are more restricted on where you work; these are usually more of an on-location atmosphere.

Pattern Making

If you really enjoy the engineering of patterns, you could always offer your services to other fashion designers. Many designers do not sew or know pattern making. They sketch their ideas and then need to hire the rest out. Creating an original pattern for a designer can bring in hundreds of dollars, which would be a great way to create addition revenue while you are getting your business going. If you are proficient in computer-aided design (CAD) software, the extra income possibilities can be endless. If you can expand your pattern-making skills to include grading, which is altering a base size pattern up and down in size, there are even more opportunities. This service could be offered to not only fashion designers but independent pattern makers that create and sell patterns to the home-sewing industry.

To find designers looking for pattern makers, check out the listings in *Women's Wear Daily*; you can even notify the fashion department at your local college. Fashion Group International (www.fgi.org) has an extensive job board for members on their website called the "Executive Job Bank." Although they are based in New York, they have resources around the country. The Association of Sewing and Design Professionals website (www.paccprofessionals.org) also allows you to list your pattern-making skills, amongst other sewing and design skills.

Sample Maker

A good sample maker can charge top dollar for their talents. As with a pattern maker, many fashion designers are in need of a sample maker. A sample maker takes the designer's pattern and sews up the garment. The first sample allows the designer to see if changes need to be made in the fit or design of the garment. The final sample garment will be used by the designer to generate sales.

There are many places to look for sample- and pattern-making opportunities (check the appendix for contact information):

- *Women's Wear Daily*
- Fashion Group International (FGI)
- Apparel Industry Board (AIBI)
- Fashion Business International (FBI)
- Fashion design colleges
- LinkedIn

Wardrobe Planning and Fashion Consulting

Personal stylists are becoming more popular with the help of shows like Bravo's *The Rachel Zoe Project* and TLC's *What Not to Wear*. Wardrobe planning and fashion consulting is a huge business. As with alterations and custom apparel, once you do a good job for a few clients, referrals will flood your way.

Do You Have the Eye?

If you have an eye for what looks good on certain body shapes and enjoy matching clothing to a client's image, this profession can be fun. Fashion consulting is not only about keeping the image of your client up to date but also making sure they are wearing styles that flatter their individual shape.

Closet Cleanout

Wardrobe planning has become a very popular business. Many women cannot determine what they need to get rid of in their closet. Not only that, but there are usually a few piles of clothes that don't fit, clothes that do not match anything, and just plain outdated clothes, and they want another opinion. In this profession you need to be perfectly honest with your client about clothing. They are paying you for your expertise. If they try on a skirt that makes them look short and wide, you need to tell them that—just maybe not in those exact words. If the skirt is salvageable by hemming it to a shorter length and tapering it for a more flattering look, let them know these options. Again, be confident in the fact that you are the expert.

If you also do alterations, you can ease your clients stress by handling the garments that can be altered, while at the same time increasing your revenue.

There are numerous books, magazine articles, and blogs out there on closet organization and styling. As far as making money, charge an hourly fee plus travel time. Any alterations you do would be a separate transaction. If you do not do alterations, consider pinning the clothes for your client and then dropping them off at the tailor shop—just an extra personal touch.

Wine and Fashion Parties

A fun way to make addition money while building your reputation as a wardrobe consultant is by having a party. I began to realize some women either could not afford the time or the money for a personal stylist, so I came up with the idea of wine and fashion parties. Think of a Pampered Chef party or a jewelry-making party; the idea is that one girl hosts the party and invites a handful of friends—usually not more than ten. Each guest is instructed to bring a few pieces of clothing that they have questions about or new styles they would like advice on. They book my time for a minimum of two hours, and I travel to the host's house.

I bring a stash of colored fabric, and each guest starts by holding up fabric to her face for a quick lesson on color analysis. Moving on to styling, one guest comes out wearing their outfit of question, and I explain how the garment should fit and what to wear with it. All of the guests learn from each other.

These parties are a great way to meet new potential clients and continue to get your name out there. I always bring the host a bottle of wine or a small gift. Many of the guests will then book future parties at their houses.

Extra Income

Although being a stylist can be a full-time profession, it is also a great way to add cash flow while you are building your sewing and fashion business. If you do alterations and you have an eye for styling and fashion, this is a fantastic way to increase your business and build a reputation.

Focus

When you first start out, it is tempting to accept any and all design and sewing jobs that come your way. Through time you will build confidence in your work, and you will begin to focus on what you are good at. Once you discover your niche, you will know exactly what jobs to consider and which ones to turn down immediately without another thought. It is important to understand that it is okay to say no.

You CANNOT Be Everything to Everyone!

This was probably one of the hardest lessons to learn. Not only does this relate to sewing and design jobs that come your way but also for your clothing line. Make a sign and hang it on your door: I CANNOT BE EVERYTHING TO EVERYONE!

While my main focus was on custom apparel, my clientele ranged in age from thirty-five to seventy-five—try making that whole group happy at the same time! After one of my first fashion shows I received comments from my older clients asking for more traditional apparel, my plus-size clients wanted larger models on the runway, and my younger clients wanted more evening wear.

Still new in my business and wanting to please everyone, I took all of these suggestions into consideration. The following year I held a fashion show using women of various ages and sizes. That would not be a bad idea if I was focusing on a ready-to-wear line, but I only did custom. Not only did I choose many diverse women to model, I designed three outfits specifically for each woman as if she were a client. I thought this would be a great way to show my expertise on styling women; it was, and the fashion show turned out fabulous. The problem is that I changed my entire aesthetic to try and make everyone happy. This show took a lot of time and money, and in the end I was left with custom-size sample garments that only fit the particular models. Although I did gain business from that show, do you know that I still received comments wanting younger, older, larger, and smaller models? The moral of the story: Stay true to your design aesthetic, focus on your plan, and know you cannot please everyone.

Narrow Your Plan

Even if you are not sure what you want to focus on right away, as time goes by you will realize what you enjoy doing. The good news is that it only takes a few jobs that you detest in order to find out what you do not want to specialize in. The busier you become, the more important it is to narrow your focus. There is only so much time in a day, so focus on what you are good at and continue to improve your skills in that particular area. It is better to strive for perfection in one area than to be mediocre in several areas.

If you are anything like me when I started my fashion design business, you are dying to jump right in and get started. I have taken special care in this chapter to load you with useful information and money-saving tips in regard to designing your collection and sourcing fabric, all the way to finishing off with a professional photo shoot. This is the chapter that you will want to come back to over and over, so pull out your highlighter.

Designing a Collection

Designing your own collection requires more than simply sketching beautiful clothes. There are many pieces to the puzzle that need to come together in order to create not only an entire collection but clothing that will sell. Try to limit the number of designs in your first collection to between twelve and fifteen. It is better to have a smaller line with fabulous pieces; this will be a little easier on your budget as well.

Before you begin sourcing fabric or even sketching, you should have already researched the market in order to determine which price point your collection will fall into. This price point needs to stay in the forefront as you design each outfit. For example, if you are keeping your designs within a range of $300 and you find a fabulous fabric that runs $75 a yard, you cannot design a garment to sell for $300 and make a profit. There are design choices that can help alter the price up or down, like designing a simple style to pair with the more expensive fabric and vice versa. It is better to know up front that your design and fabric choices are not coming in at a profit so you can adjust accordingly.

Focus

By now you have also determined who your ideal client is going to be, so you should begin to piece together what you think that client will buy and what style range you want your collection to fall into. Start by laying out your designs and ideas. Many times these ideas might be all over the map, and now is the time to narrow your focus and vision for your collection. Do you see a common theme in your ideas and sketches or is there something you specialize in that you can narrow in on?

For example, if you lay out all your sketches and see a plethora of evening gowns, jeans, workout jackets, and swimsuits, technically you are dealing with four totally different collections. You need to pick one collection to focus on. Always keeping in mind your client, price points, overall style, and any other factors that you think are important. There might be styles you need to discard or items you need to add, but it is important to start with a focused overall concept in order to create a cohesive collection. Again, keep in mind that you cannot be everything to everyone!

Creating a Storyboard

A storyboard is simply a collection for pictures, prints, fabrics, and anything else that you might draw inspiration from. I must admit, I thoroughly enjoy creating storyboards. In fact, they are all over my studio; some focus on my collection of the time and others with general ideas to fall back on. I have a wall with evening-wear inspiration that includes different beading ideas, various neckline draping, and fabric samples. Jackets are one of my signatures, so I also have a board with ideas for fabric manipulations, custom trim options, hand-dyed lining samples, various collar samples, and so on. I even have a storyboard with advertising ideas that include snippets from my favorite magazine ads, quotes, pictures, model poses, and layouts.

A storyboard is a great place to start with ideas for your collection. Where is your inspiration going to come from? This could be anything from a certain period of time, a building, a picture, even a trip you recently took. Most of my inspiration comes from fabric so I usually start collecting particular fabrics I want to work with that season, along with choosing a color theme. I might hand dye select pieces and topstitch others, then add sample trims and embellishments to the board. From there I will sketch styles and ideas that transpire from the actual materials.

Here are examples of two of my storyboards
for inspiration.

Inspiration

Inspiration for your line can come from many places and resources. Styles might reflect a particular historical or cultural era that transpires from history books, old movies, or vintage clothing, to name just a few. There might even be one style that inspires your entire collection. Looking for inspiration? Visit high-end boutiques or the designer floor at Barney's. Browse fashion magazines, visit Style.com, and scan the runway shows, or visit a large fabric store. Fabric trade shows are also an ideal place for inspiration—my personal favorite.

Designing a Cohesive Collection

If you plan on selling your clothing line to a store or online through your own website, it is important to design a cohesive collection. A cohesive collection means that each garment not only looks great by itself, but all the garments together look good and work as an entire collection. Take a glance at your sketches and then consider how your clothes will look hanging on a rack together. The colors, the overall theme, and the styles must complement one another. As mentioned earlier, you cannot have a rack of evening gowns with yoga pants. It is very obvious both styles are totally unrelated, and a store buyer would laugh you out the door. What is not so obvious is color palette, proportion, and theme, all while keeping your ideal client in mind. Ask yourself the following questions:

1. Are the colors complementary?
2. Can pieces in the collections be worn together?
3. Do the garments fit the image of your client?
4. Are the styles cohesive?
5. If this collection was hanging on a rack in a retail store, does it look good together?
6. Does my collection tell a story?

Sketching

Sketching is more than a beautiful piece of art. Sketching your designs helps to work out any design kinks while taking an overall look at your collection. I usually sketch the fashion model with the garment first, and then when the design is finalized I prepare a flat sketch.

Fashion sketch: While you are formulating your designs you need to sketch the garment on a model. Usually you sketch the garment from the front and the back. Don't worry, even if sketching is not your forte, there are a lot of free sketching tools online. I have never been able to get the body proportions correct, so I took a class by Carol Kimball (www.carolkimball.net) that taught me how to sketch with a croquis. *Croquis* means simply "sketch" in French. In fashion, the term refers to a quick sketch of a figure. Another website I found to be very helpful, which also includes downloads (many free) for croquis, templates, and sketching ideas, is DesignersNexus.com.

Sample Croquis

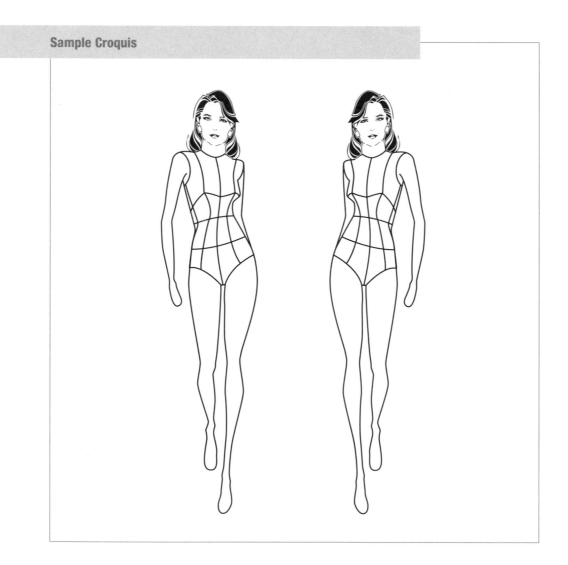

Flat sketch: A flat sketch is used in order to portray your garment in detail. Flat sketching is used for pattern layout, technical details on the design, as well as line sheets. To start, include a two-dimensional sketch from the front, back, and possibly the side that contains pattern details including seams, topstitching, and design particulars.

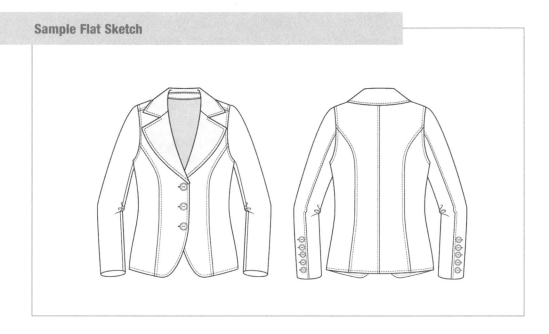

Nowadays most flat sketching is done on a computer using Illustrator, Corel-Draw, Adobe Photoshop, or some form of digital fashion design software. I originally purchased a software package called Digital Fashion Pro from StartingaClothingLine .com and was pleased to find this software user friendly and not too expensive; they now use Inkscape for their software program. Many of my first years of designing with this software were fine, but once I began designing patterns with CAD software, I needed Adobe Illustrator. Just make sure you keep all your design needs in mind when choosing a software program. If you are undecided, Illustrator is the fashion design go-to for software, and if you decide to work for another designer, Illustrator is a *must*. Now, do not be discouraged by the price of Illustrator. If you are a student, they offer a discount, and they also offer rental fees for those of us that are past the student era.

Fabric and Trim Sourcing

It is important to understand the fiber content of different fabrics and how the fiber content relates to care, quality, and wear. By understanding textiles you will have a better concept of what fabrics work for certain styles. For example a silk dupioni is not the best choice for a soft, wrap dress, and a slinky knit is not ideal for a tailored jacket. There are numerous books on textiles and fabric content, one of my favorites is *Claire Shaeffer's Fabric Sewing Guide*. Visiting a fabric store is another great way to begin to understand fabric. Analyze the texture, drape, and thickness of each fabric type. Create a notebook of your favorite fabric swatches along with a detailed description about fiber content and care. The swatch book can be a great reference for years to come.

As a new designer, it can be challenging ordering wholesale fabric because of the minimum yardage required by many of these suppliers. Check out AboutSources .com. They have a resource guide called "The Designer's Guide" that lists numerous fabric and trim sources for the smaller designer. They also list many of the companies on their website.

Online Fabric Sourcing

The Internet can supply you with numerous fabric options at your fingertips. There are so many fabric stores online, including both wholesale and retail, that you will

In a three-ring binder create a fabric reference book by inserting sheets with the following details on each fabric to keep track of your ideas:

- Fabric swatch
- Name of fabric
- Name of supplier
- SKU #
- Re-orderable   yes   no
- Price per yard
- Fabric width
- Brief description of fiber content
- Care instructions
- Style ideas

	Swatch of Fabric:
Supplier: London Textiles **Phone:** 800-431-6647 **Contact:** Ricki USA	
SKU # 4671-342 **Name of fabric (optional):** **Content:** 65% wool, 30% rayon, 5% spandex	
Price per yard: $18.95	
Fabric width: 56"	
Care instructions: dry clean only **Additional notes:** Order over 50 yards for price break.	**Description and style ideas:** Lightweight wool, beautiful drape, perfect for any slacks style.

quickly find a few favorites. Once you find a few suppliers, build a relationship with those businesses. Many of the online retail sites offer discounts for a business. They also offer special discounts through e-mail, so make sure you sign up for their e-mail newsletters. Also make sure you monitor shipping charges closely; these need to be added to your fabric bottom-line cost.

It is challenging to order fabric online because the picture on the website might not portray the actual color or drape of the fabric. If you are looking at a wholesale site, they will often send you a color card for a particular fabric. This really makes a difference, because then you can feel the actual fabric and see the variety of color choices firsthand. When ordering from a retail site, they will usually offer fabric swatches for a minimal fee.

Once you find the fabrics for your collection, you need to find out if the fabric can be reordered. If not, you want to know up front, before you design your entire collection. You will also need to check if the fabric has any designer ties that would prevent you from using the fabric in your garment for resale; if so, you will usually see the designer's name or logo down the selvage of the fabric.

Here are a few favorite websites to start with. Make sure to set up a business wholesale account as some of these also offer retail pricing:

- VogueFabricsStore.com
- FabricMartFabrics.com
- Fashiondex.com
- AboutSources.com
- FTWFabric.com
- RichlinFabrics.com
- ElliottBermanTextiles.com
- HabermanFabrics.com

Retail Stores

Price points can be a challenge when shopping at a retail fabric store, but the good news is that many of them offer a business discount if you supply them with a copy of your sales tax ID number and a business license. Again, it is important to build relationships with the stores you are going to frequent. Introduce yourself and explain that you are a new fashion designer, and most of the owners will be thrilled to assist in anyway.

Even if the retail store is out of your area, they might have a website for reference, or you can always call them and describe what you are looking for. They can send you swatches, and then you can go from there. Again, be sure to find out if the fabric can be reordered and if there are any restrictions on using the fabric in your collection.

Fabric and Trim Shows

Even if you are not ready to purchase from wholesalers, mills, or jobbers, there is no better experience than visiting a fabric and trim show. These shows take place around the world, and they offer priceless information on upcoming fabric and color trends. This is where you will eventually base your fabric sourcing.

You can go WeConnectFashion.com or ApparelNews.net and download the current trade show calendar, which also displays the smaller shows that might be in your area. Both sites offer a link with each event for sign-up information.

The fabric trade shows are held twice a year, with the largest shows being Premier Vision in Paris and Texworld in New York City. If you take a look at the calendar, you will find smaller fabric shows in other cities and states, including Chicago, Dallas, and California. I usually attend the Chicago Fabric and Trim show; although the show is smaller than Texworld, it allows me to narrow in on the suppliers that carry what I need. These shows can be a little overwhelming at first, so stay focused on what you are looking for. If you purchase fabric right then at the show, keep your budget and collection in mind at all times.

When you go to a show, do not be embarrassed because you are just starting out; act professional and know what to ask for. Find out what their minimums are. You will discover that many of the vendors have minimums too high for you to even consider at this time, so narrow in on the places that will cater to smaller designers such as yourself. There are some who will sell a minimum of twenty yards, along with offering sample yardage.

The supplier will usually offer sample yardage of three to five yards, or however many yards of fabric you need to create the samples in your collection. You probably do not need fifty yards of the same fabric for your samples, so this is an inexpensive way to create your collection, and then you will reorder once your line sells. The sample yardage is more expensive than when you reorder the fabric in a larger quantity, so make sure you take note of both prices.

True Story

My very first fabric and trim show was an expensive learning adventure, and I am only sharing this so you do not make the same mistake. When I arrived at the show, I really did not have a plan of action as I was not familiar with any of the suppliers and really had absolutely no clue how this whole trade show really worked. All I did know was that I could view fabric from all over the world in one location; what could possibly go wrong? I spent hours browsing through fabric swatches going from vendor to vendor, I met quite a few reps (that I actually still do business with today), and I made invaluable contacts for future ordering. There is nothing wrong with just viewing and scoping things out. The problem came about when I decided to purchase fabric without a focused collection in mind or a strict budget to follow. At the time, I only designed one-of-a-kind custom apparel. I remember looking at a gorgeous piece of royal-blue raw silk, thinking it would make a fabulous jacket, and then onto a teal silk dupioni: "This would make a gorgeous mother of the bride suit." Are you getting the idea? When it came time to order, I simply filled in my address and business information. The vendor scribbled a few numbers, and off I went to the next booth.

Well, this was over fifteen years ago, and the preferred form of payment was COD (cash on delivery). When I got home, I laid out all the yellow and pink receipts with a calculator. I had ordered over $12,000 of fabric! I called each vendor to find out the date of delivery and was thrilled to hear that half of the fabric would not be delivered for over a month. Needless to say, the next few months seemed like Christmas with fabric arriving just about every week. Some of the fabric I was thrilled with, and others made me shake my head and wonder what I was thinking. I was *not* thinking, and that was the problem. I ended up with a number of ten- to twenty-yard bolts of fabric in every color and texture. Put it this way, if I worked for a designer and we were trying to create a cohesive collection, I would have been fired immediately.

Never again did I go to a show and simply order off the cuff. Instead I would bring along a list of the fabrics, sample yardage, and colors I needed at the time. I also had a list for fabrics to research later, and I would get information from the vendor and request swatch cards.

Trade Show Tips

Here are a few tips to keep in mind when attending a trade show:

1. Carry your business card to hand out.
2. Bring a copy of your sales tax ID number.
3. Bring a copy of your employer identification number (EIN).
4. Collect business cards from potential suppliers.
5. Carry a notebook for notes.
6. Stay organized.
7. Stay FOCUSED!

Payment Terms

Once you build a relationship with some of the suppliers, many of them will offer you terms such as net 30, net 60, or net 90. This means you have 30, 60, or 90 days to pay in full. Some might offer you a discount if you pay within 15 days. For example: A company offers you a 4 percent discount if you pay within 15 days. This is how it will look on your bill: 4/15 net 30.

I have also noticed that a few companies add 4.5 percent to the bill if paying with a credit card. Sending a check seems so old-fashioned, but when it affects your bottom line, it is a good idea to break out your checkbook.

Inspect the Fabric

When your fabric arrives, be sure to lay out the entire bolt in order to check for flaws and discoloration. If there is a problem you need to let the supplier know *immediately*. After you cut into the fabric, it is too late. I received an entire bolt of black rayon viscose that had pieced fabric throughout the entire bolt, meaning the fabric had been cut and stitched together many times to fill the bolt instead of being one continuous piece. If I had not checked the bolt before cutting, I would have lost a lot of money trying to cut around these flaws. If you have your fabric sent directly to a factory for cutting, make sure they are instructed to inspect the fabric as well.

Jobbers

Jobbers are individuals that purchase larger quantities of left over fabric from mills and manufacturers. The fabric is typically mill overruns, odd lots, and seconds, meaning the quality might not have been what the original designer had requested. The jobber then turns around and sells the fabric at wholesale prices to stores and smaller designers, or they have a retail outlet of their own, like Vogue Fabrics and Fabric Mart. You might consider purchasing your fabric from a jobber, because the minimums are very low, even as small as one yard, which is well within a small designer's budget. The jobber will usually charge a premium for their fabrics, but it is still less expensive than retail pricing, and this is your chance to purchase from some of the larger mills that you would otherwise have to pass on. Just be sure to do some checking:

- Make sure the fabric is not outdated.
- Check the fabric for flaws.
- Confirm that the fabric is not already saturating the market from other major designers.
- Verify that there are not any copyright or designer logos attached to the fabric.

I purchase from jobbers quite frequently, especially when I am working on a custom garment or a specific project, always keeping in the back of my mind that the odds of reordering the same fabric down the line are pretty limited. But you can ask them how much of a certain fabric they have available, and they will tell you.

As you grow as a designer, you might consider selling your excess fabric to a jobber.

I have listed a few of my favorite jobbers (see page 53). It does not matter where they are located because you just call them and list the fabrics and colors that you are looking for, and they will send swatches. You order from the swatches and you will usually receive the fabric within a few days.

Mills

A mill manufactures fabrics and textile products. The word *mill* refers to the building that much of the spinning, knitting, weaving, and so on are completed in. The minimums are quite high when ordering from a mill, usually over one thousand yards. If you are ordering from a mill, be sure to check the lead time, which is the time it takes you to receive your fabric from the time you place the order.

Do not totally disregard all mills if you are looking for a special fabric or knitting. One of my fabric wholesalers referred me to a mill that would manufacture a special fabric specifically for me, and they allowed me to purchase three hundred yards as a minimum. You can find an index of mills at Fashiondex.com.

Wholesalers

A wholesaler purchases excess fabrics from mills, converters, and large apparel manufacturers, and in return they sell to smaller manufacturers and retail fabric stores. You will usually be able to order smaller quantities than you can from the mill itself; just be sure to check the quantity of fabric available before your purchase. If they have a closeout with minimal yardage, you want to know that before you order. At first you will most likely work with a rep instead of the wholesaler directly,

Wholesaler Resources

These are two of my favorites wholesalers:

Richlin Fabrics Inc.
414 E. 14th Ave.
North Kansas City, MO 64116
(800) 742-4546
richlinfabrics.com

Telio Montreal
625 Deslauriers
Montreal, QC H4N 1W8
(800) 361-0375
telio.com

Telio Toronto
219 Dufferin St.
Suite 106A
Toronto, ON M6K 1Y9
(800) 361-0375
telio.com

Telio Vancouver
211 Columbia St.
Suite 212
Vancouver, BC V6A 2R5
(800) 361-0375
telio.com

especially if you are buying smaller quantities. If there is a company that you order from frequently, you will find the wholesaler name and contact information on the side of the fabric bolts; you can always call them yourself. In fact, I was introduced to some of the wholesalers that I work with now from working with sales reps. Maybe the rep does not carry the line from the wholesaler any longer, and that is a perfect reason to contact the wholesaler directly. Trade shows and online sources (www.fashiondex.com, www.aboutsources.com) are another good place to start looking for a wholesaler.

Some wholesalers also sell their fabrics through their websites. As I mentioned earlier, it can be challenging ordering online, so make sure you ask for swatches or sample cards. The minimum orders vary, but typically you will need to purchase full bolts and a minimum dollar amount.

Reps

Sales reps represent select mills, and they work with manufacturers and designers in a select territory. If you find reps who carry fabrics that you like and they are willing to sell in smaller lots, you will want to build a relationship with them. They are your contact for new fabrics, and you can always call them and let them know what you are looking for. Some of the mills they represent will require larger minimums on fabric orders, but many of them will be more than happy to assist you with your first collections by providing sample yardage.

Sales Rep Resource

Chicago Wholesale Fabrics
2256 W. Grand Ave.
Chicago, IL 60612
(708) 386-8586
chicagowholesalefabrics.com

Retailer/Jobber/Wholesaler Resources

The combination of retailer, jobber, and wholesaler can be a great resource for a new designer because of the small quantities and their price points. I have listed five of the places I have worked with for years. They each have retail outlets either in a store or online and you can set up wholesale accounts for better pricing.

Elliott Berman Textiles
225 W. 35th St.
7th Floor
New York, NY 10001
(800) 609-6072
elliottbermantextiles.com

Fabric Mart
Retail outlet
3911 Penn Ave.
Sinking Spring, PA 19608
(800) 242-3695
fabricmartfabrics.com

Fishman's Fabrics
1101 South Desplaines St.
Chicago, IL 60607
(312) 922-7250
fishmansfabrics.com

Richlin Fabrics
414 E. 14th Ave.
North Kansas City, MO 64116
(800) 742-4546
richlinfabrics.com

Availability of Fabric

You have orders, but the fabric is no longer available, now what? Even if you check the fabric availability at the time you order your sample yardage, it does not guarantee the fabric will be available in a few months when you are ready to start production with orders at hand. This has happened to many small designers, including myself, so do not be discouraged if it happens to you. First, you will need to resource an alternative fabric that is as close to the original as possible. Next, contact the buyers that placed orders with you and explain what happened. Show them the alternative fabric that you have found and see if they are still on board with their order. Lastly, it is a good idea to have the buyer sign a form confirming their approval with the new fabric. Do not under any circumstance switch the fabrics without prior approval from the store buyer.

I have read many times that a new designer should keep their fabric selection simple and avoid wild prints. The main reasoning is that if you design your samples based around a printed fabric but you cannot order that fabric when the time comes, you risk wasting your entire line. This happened to me one season. After attending a fabric trade show, I purchased sample yardage of a printed silk charmeuse. The fabric was going to be a main part of my collection: lining for my jackets and coordinating tops. I asked the wholesaler how much of this fabric was available and wanted some confirmation that in six weeks I would be able to reorder since there would be a high possibility I would need more fabric if the collection was the success I was hoping it would be. He confirmed that there was quite a bit of this fabric available, and if I reordered even within eight weeks he did not foresee a problem. I finished my samples in four weeks and invited some select clients to view the collection before the trunk show. With preorders in hand I called the wholesaler, and much to my dismay, the fabric was no longer available. Half of my collection was based on this print, and I was not able to take any orders!

Creating Samples

Now that you have solidified your designs and your fabric is selected, it is time to create your samples. You will have a sample made of each design in your collection, and these samples are what you will show to a potential buyer in order to generate sales. If you are outsourcing, most factories and contractors will charge a premium rate for your first sample and then discount the price tremendously for actual orders. By doing this, they hope to prevent you from using them for the samples and then sending your larger order overseas for manufacturing.

Each sample will probably require a few fittings, resulting in changes to the pattern or design in order to perfect the fit. If you have pattern-making, fitting, and sewing skills, you can save yourself quite a bit of money creating your own first samples. With that said, be realistic about your sewing skills. Can you sew a garment that looks like it came off a retail floor? If not, you will need to have the sewing process hired out to a professional until your skills are up to par. Your samples represent your collection. They need to be well made.

Pattern Making

If there is one skill you should try to master, it should be understanding pattern-making and fit. There are so many designers that do not understand the engineering that goes into constructing a pattern, and many times this results in poor fit or a design that just will not work. Even if your sewing skills are limited, you can still test your own patterns with a muslin. This will allow you to go back and forth with your pattern design until the fit is perfect.

Hiring a Pattern Maker

If you decide to hire someone to do your pattern making, make sure you check their references, scrutinize their experience, and ask to see some of their samples. Pricing differs according to the complexity of the pattern, but you will want to confirm that it includes making adjustments to the pattern with fitting issues. Start by testing them with one design to make sure they can deliver what they promise, all while keeping an eye on the turnaround time. Lastly, check that they do not share your patterns or designs with anyone else.

Making Your Own Patterns

If you will be doing your own pattern making, here are a few fantastic books to use as reference: *Patternmaking for Fashion Design* and *Draping for Apparel Design,* both by Helen Joseph-Armstrong, and *Patternmaking Made Easy, The Art of Fashion Draping,* and *Grading Workbook,* all by Connie Amaden-Crawford.

These books are filled with everything you will need to know for pattern making and draping, and they are also a great resource for inspiration. While designing your patterns, check the fit of each style. You need a fit model who has the exact measurements for each particular size that you plan to manufacture. Ask the model to walk, sit, and move around; analyze how the garment looks on the model. Check for movement restriction or unsightly wrinkles due to improper fit, and make your adjustments to the pattern accordingly. Continue the fitting and altering process until the pattern fits just the way you like. As tempting as it is to be your own fit model, it is better to use someone else.

CAD (Computer-Aided Design) Software

Advancements in technology have really paved the way to efficiency in the overall fashion-design industry. If you are at all familiar with CAD software, you know what I am talking about when it comes to pattern making. Although the price tag on this software package can be expensive, the ease of use and time-saving applications help it pay for itself quickly. There are many different brands of CAD software to choose, and they range in price from $700 to over $10,000 for basic flat pattern designing, grading, and marking. The price continues up as you get into the 3-D pattern drafting, which is an incredible addition to the traditional CAD software. The new 3-D addition allows you to see how your garment will look on an actual model; in fact, the model can spin and even walk down a runway. Changes to your pattern are simple: If you want to change a seam placement, just move the line and the pattern alters itself. You can imagine how much time this could save a designer, and hopefully in time the 3-D version will become more affordable as well. If you are proficient in computers and mathematics, it will definitely be worth your while to research some of these software programs, especially as your company grows.

I currently use two different CAD software programs. I started with Pattern Maker (www.patternmakerusa.com) many years ago; this software was pretty easy to learn and cost under $1,000. You can also purchase additional garments to use as a base pattern, which is really helpful when you are getting started. The other program, called MacroGen, allows you to custom-size your patterns. I can input a client's measurements and choose a pattern and the pattern will print to their measurements. If you are focusing on custom apparel I highly recommend this software for that application. Now, this does not mean you can skip on learning pattern making and fitting; the patterns do not always come out perfect, and you will probably need to make some adjustments. But on the positive side, this can save you hours when designing for an individual client. This software has come out with a few updates through the years, and I was always able to download the new version at no additional cost.

When I made the business decision to design a pattern collection for the home sewer, I decided to upgrade to a better CAD system. After researching a few big names I decided to go with Optitex (www.optitex.com). They offer 24/7 customer service, personal training, excellent tutorials, and you can rent or purchase the software. After six hours of personal training I was up and running, and I am thrilled with the ease of use. This is one of the few CAD software programs that runs on Windows, so the learning curve is really easy. Optitex also offers 3-D designing capabilities, which I have not upgraded to as of yet, but I am drooling at the possibilities.

Have you ever heard the saying that you get what you pay for? Well, that speaks volumes when it comes to pattern-making software. In regards to customer service, training, and user-friendly software, the higher price is worth every penny. Refer to the quick checklist on page 61 while researching pattern-making software companies.

Grading and Marking

After drafting your patterns, the next step is to grade your patterns. Grading is the process of adjusting your patterns up and down in sizing. The United States does not have a national standard on sizing, but you should try to maintain consistency within

❏ Does the software include pattern making, grading, and marking?

❏ As your company grows, are you able to add features?

❏ Can you use your current computer?

❏ Do you need to purchase additional hard-drive space?

❏ Do they offer a lease-to-own program?

❏ If you purchase the software, do you have to pay for updates, or is there an annual maintenance fee?

❏ Do they offer a free trial period?

❏ How long does it usually take customer service to respond to your question or problem?

❏ Do they offer phone support?

❏ Do they have 24/7 support?

❏ Are there online tutorials?

❏ Can you pay extra for one-on-one training?

❏ Is there a manual you can download?

In commenting on the customer support, 24/7 online support is worth its weight in gold if you have tight deadlines.

your collections from year to year. Regardless if you choose to grade the patterns yourself or hire that process out, make sure you check the fit of each size especially with your first few collections. Instead of creating a finished sample in each size, simply sew up a muslin with inexpensive fabric to check the fit.

Here are a few books that I found helpful to understanding grading and sizing:

- *Grading Workbook* by Connie Amaden-Crawford
- *The Apparel Design and Production Handbook* by the Fashiondex
- *Grading Techniques for Fashion Design* by Jeanne Price and Bernard Zamkoff

There are professional graders that you can send your pattern out to for the entire grading process, and the cost is not very expensive. Even if you do your pattern designing with CAD software, there are many pattern-making experts that you can rely on. As a new designer you are probably tight on funds, but at the same time you can only do so much. If you are not familiar with the grading process, this would be a job to send out.

Marking is the process of organizing all of your pattern pieces in the most economical cutting layout possible. If you are designing your patterns on a CAD software system, you can do this with no problem, otherwise there are services to send this out to as well. At first you might not see the importance of marking, but the more fabric you can save will ultimately save you money in the long run.

Cutting

If you are selling on a smaller scale you can easily cut the fabric yourself; in fact, many of the smaller sewing contractors want the pattern pieces already cut and bundled. You will definitely want a tabletop 60 inches wide and at least 10 feet long—the longer, the better in order to cut many patterns out of one fabric layout. The fabrics and styles you are cutting will determine if you cut each pattern individually or if you layer the fabric in order to cut multiple patterns at once. If you layer rows of fabric for cutting multiple patterns, keep the grain line in mind at all times, and make sure a full garment is cut with each layer in case of dye lot changes. A dye lot is a number given to a group of fabrics that are dyed together, which is important to pay attention to. You can purchase six bolts of fabric, but if they are not the same dye lot there can be a slight variation in tint or shading. Label the cut pattern pieces and keep each style together until it's time to sew. If you will be sending this cut fabric to a sewing contractor you will need to bundle each garment with the labeled pattern pieces, thread, and any notions such as zippers and buttons.

If you plan on hiring out the cutting, check with your sewing contractor about whom they would recommend. The website Fashiondex.com also has a list of contractors. If you want your clothing made in Chicago, the Apparel Industry Board (www.aibi.com) has a great resource of contractors, and they are dedicated to helping the smaller designer. Check your area for similar resources.

Sewing

Manufacturing your own clothes is not out of the question as a small designer. You will need to sew fast, while maintaining high standards in quality. There is a book and class offered by Islander Sewing Systems (www.islandersewing.com) that teaches the sewing techniques and shortcuts in the garment industry. Again, you need to be realistic about your sewing skills. Can you produce a professional-looking garment? If not then either improve on those skills or you need to hire contractors.

Manufacturing License

If you live in New York State or California, you will need to obtain a license from the state Department of Labor before you can manufacture your own apparel. The license has an annual fee of $200 in New York with a renewal of $150 per year. California fees are a little steeper, ranging from $750 to $2,500. See the websites below for application details. Even though those are the only two states requiring a license at this time, laws are always changing, so check with your state to make sure there are not any stipulations for manufacturing apparel.

- New York: www.labor.state.ny.us/workerProtection/LaborStandards/workprot/garment.asp
- California: www.dir.ca.gov/databases/dlselr/garmreg.html

These licenses are required in both states, even if you are a one-person shop. The California government states that "every person engaged in the business of garment manufacturing must register with the Labor Commissioner." They go on to describe a "person" as an "individual, partnership, corporation, [or] limited liability." Then, if you have any doubt, they solidify the need for a license by explaining "garment manufacturing" as "sewing, cutting, making, processing, repairing, finishing, assembling, or otherwise preparing any garment or any article of wearing apparel or accessories designed or intended as a person, to be worn by an individual, including, but not limited to, clothing, hats, gloves, handbags, hosiery, ties, scarves, and belts, for sale or resale by any person or any persons contracting to have these operations performed."

Hiring Yourself

As a small, self-employed designer you will find yourself doing everything at first. From the initial designing to pinning on hangtags, you are the one who is trying to make your business successful. If you are sewing all the garments or even just the sample garments, you need to come up with an hourly work rate for yourself. Even if you are unable to pay yourself right away, eventually your business is going to grow, and you will be hiring contractors to do the sewing. If you have discounted your time too much or not accounted for it at all, your pricing is going to be inaccurate, and you will not be able to afford to hire anyone.

Hiring a Contractor

When the time comes to hire a contractor or factory to manufacture your apparel, there are many resources to find the right match for your product. Interview the contractor, find out what kind of work they do and what type of product they specialize in. Visit the factory or studio. Are they using professional equipment? What type of work atmosphere do their employees work in? Is the place clean and organized? Ask to see some of the finished garments they are currently working on and inspect the quality closely.

Quality Control

Once you have chosen a contractor and begin working together, visit the factory often. As a small designer with minimal orders, there is a tendency for your garments to be pushed aside if a larger order comes their way. Another reason to keep tabs on the production process is to monitor the quality. If there is a mistake during construction, you will notice this immediately during an inspection, and mistakes can be corrected. I have read horror stories about designers receiving their final product only to find something majorly wrong. By then it's too late to adjust an order and make the deadline for delivering to the stores. Can you imagine opening up your boxes with jackets that are to be delivered in a week and finding all the jackets sewn with plastic zippers instead of metal? Such a simple mistake: The trim supplier mailed the wrong zippers to the contractor, the contractor just sews what they have in hand, and you are the one out of luck with a costly mistake. Quality control is of utmost importance when hiring contractors for any job.

Manufacturing Overseas

As a designer starting out, having your garments manufactured overseas creates an even greater challenge. The price might be right, but you will need to either visit the factory yourself or hire someone to monitor the production process. I have heard of designers receiving perfectly sewn, high-quality first samples from a factory overseas, only to have the final product show up looking nothing like the original samples.

Photo Shoot

Planning a photo shoot is a lot of fun, and seeing your clothing on a model in print is even more exciting. There are usually two types of pictures that come from a photo shoot:

- Pictures to sell the garments.
- Pictures for an ad or promo.

Consider the difference of a photo ad in *Elle* magazine compared to the same item for sale on the Nordstrom website. If you click on the Nordstrom site you will see a picture of the garment for sale, shot with a simple gray background. This allows your eye to focus on the garment for sale without any distractions. Compare that image to a print ad in a magazine. A good ad encompasses the entire lifestyle that particular brand represents. These shots are usually more glamorous and visually appealing.

Pictures to Sell Your Product

If you are shooting pictures for a look book, catalog, or e-commerce the main focus should be on the clothing itself. A simple, neutral background is ideal. I mainly use a black background for lighter-color clothing and a white or gray background for everything else.

I set up a small shooting area in my studio for this type of picture. I found a four-light photography package from Cowboy Studio on Amazon.com for under one hundred dollars and hung a large piece of fabric on a curtain rod attached to the wall. This has been an ideal layout for me and for other photographers to shoot in. I do not have to worry about finding or renting a location, and I am ready to shoot at any time.

Pictures for an Ad or Promo

These are the pictures used in ad campaigns, promotion, or for a feature on your website. The backdrops and settings are usually as intriguing as the outfits themselves. These photo shoots take more preparation and imagination because you need to encompass your entire brand image in one picture.

Finding a Photographer

There are a lot of creative photographers to choose from, so where do you start and how do you keep the cost down when you are first starting out? Check with the local schools for photography students. Many of these students are looking to build a portfolio, and they are more than happy to shoot at no charge in exchange for using the pictures for that purpose. You might also find professional photographers who are looking to expand their portfolio in the fashion industry, and that is a win-win for both of you. Make sure that you both agree that if the pictures are used by either of you, the name of the photographer and the name of the designer are typically listed in the credits along with the model's name.

Choosing Models

A local modeling agency is an easy way to find good models, but think outside of the box. Do you have any friends or relatives who have the look you need? If you find inexperienced models whom you think can work, ask if they are willing to trade modeling for the pictures. Many of these younger models are also trying to build a portfolio and would love a high-fashion picture for their résumé. Make the same deal with them as with photographers: You will include their name in the credits with the picture and they will use yours (as the designer) also.

Keeping the Photo Shoot Cost to a Minimum

When laying out a fashion shoot or even a fashion show, make a list of who might also benefit from your pictures. By doing this, you could potentially work out a deal where they can use the pictures in exchange for their services. This is particularly true for hair stylists, makeup artists, models, and photographers. Before you spend money on a location or a studio rental, is there a restaurant or furniture store that could benefit from the pictures as well? Think outside the box!

Keep these potential vendors in mind for trade:

- Professional photographer
- Model
- Florist
- Furniture store
- Makeup artist
- Hair dresser
- Shoe store
- Accessory store
- Jewelry store

Find a Location to Shoot

This is where you need to be creative. Look at buildings, roads, nature; try to find a cool background for your shot all while keeping in mind the lifestyle you are trying to portray with your brand. If the location is on private property make sure you ask for permission from the owner. If you are on city property, do a quick check to make sure you do not need a special permit.

Outdoor locations can make a gorgeous background, unless of course the weather does not cooperate. There is a lot of planning and coordinating of schedules between the model, hair and makeup, the photographer, and anyone else lending a

Photo Shoot Checklist

- ❏ Makeup
- ❏ Hairspray
- ❏ Shoes
- ❏ Jewelry
- ❏ Steamer
- ❏ Full outfits with belts or accessories
- ❏ Lint brush
- ❏ Tissues
- ❏ Clips for fitting the clothing to the model
- ❏ Mini first-aid kit
- ❏ Extra pantyhose or tights
- ❏ Strapless bra
- ❏ Bra cups
- ❏ Shoulder pads
- ❏ Safety pins
- ❏ Needle and thread

hand, so it would be a shame if the weather does not cooperate and you are forced to cancel. Instead, have another inside location as an alternative backup plan.

Preparing for the photo shoot requires organization so that you are not running back and forth from the shoot to your studio grabbing things you forgot. Use the checklist on page 68 as a quick reference for the items to pack before any shoot or fashion show.

Combining Fashion with Business

Now that you have your collection visualized, let's move on to setting up your space for business. This sounds so simple, but this is crucial to your efficiency. The first few years of my business, I felt like I could have had my own rearranging episode on HGTV. I seriously altered my furniture, equipment arrangement, and room layout at least every other month. Trust me, this was not because I was bored, but for the simple fact of making the day-to-day operations more efficient.

04 Setting Up the Space for Business

Laying out your space for business is a little more complicated than just rearranging your furniture for looks. You need to take into account your entire business, including the following:

- How many employees or contractors will you have coming and going? (This may be just you in the beginning.)
- Will you have clients visiting your home?
- Are you constricted to one small room in your house?
- Are there areas you will be sharing with your family?

When you start out, you need to do the best with what you have to work with, and efficiency is the key element for success. As your business grows you will obviously make changes, but setting up the right way and purchasing the right equipment to start off will save you time and money.

Equipment Requirements

Starting a sewing and fashion-related business should not cost you a lot of money. As your business grows you will want to add specialty machines and supplies, but you can easily start with some basic equipment.

Sewing Essentials

The layout and size of your space, not to mention your budget, will ultimately determine how you initially set up your sewing space and what equipment you purchase. Through time you might upgrade your equipment, but do not be afraid of starting with the basics. Stay focused on what you need to get started. The beautiful embroidery machines and sophisticated software will seem very appealing while you are researching sewing equipment, but if none of your garments are going to utilize embroidery, you need to skip this lavish addition. Are you getting the idea?

Sewing Machine

There are many different options when purchasing a sewing machine from speed to stitch variations to price points. Start your search by gathering a list of home sewing machines and commercial machines that are in your budget. Next make a list of what you plan on designing and sewing; this list will help to narrow the sewing machine selection down. For example, if you are going to focus on canvas handbags, you will go straight to the commercial machines.

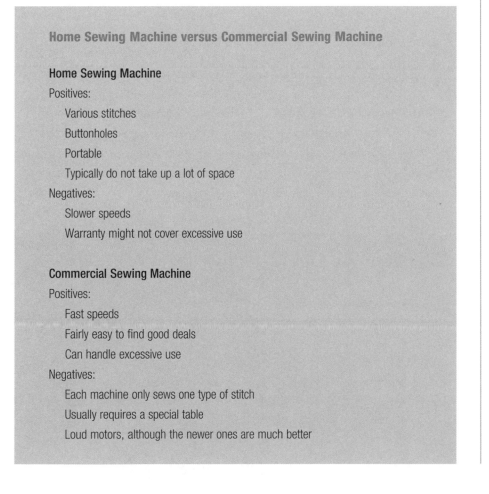

Home Sewing Machine versus Commercial Sewing Machine

Home Sewing Machine
Positives:
    Various stitches
    Buttonholes
    Portable
    Typically do not take up a lot of space
Negatives:
    Slower speeds
    Warranty might not cover excessive use

Commercial Sewing Machine
Positives:
    Fast speeds
    Fairly easy to find good deals
    Can handle excessive use
Negatives:
    Each machine only sews one type of stitch
    Usually requires a special table
    Loud motors, although the newer ones are much better

The home sewing machine will usually offer a variety of different design stitches and sewing machine feet. If you go this route, consider purchasing your machine from a local sewing shop that offers machine servicing. With the amount of sewing you will be doing, you need to have your machine cleaned once a year. For the first seven years of my business, I used a basic home sewing machine, and it worked just fine. Then came the need for speed.

Most commercial machines only sew one stitch, but they are fast and easy to use. When I started sewing jeans, a commercial machine became a necessity—although I still use my home sewing machine for buttonholes, decorative zigzag stitching on the pockets, and embroidery.

There are a few questions to ask when purchasing a commercial machine:

- How loud is the motor? Are there quieter options? (Many of the new machines have a silent motor.)
- Does it take oil?
- Does it come with a table, or is that extra?
- Do you need a special electrical outlet?

List the sewing machine stitches you think you will need for your business; this will help you narrow your search. If your budget allows, I would suggest purchasing a commercial machine for production and a basic sewing machine for the extra stitches.

I found a basic commercial sewing machine with a table for under $600. I use this machine for jeans, but it is so loud! I currently use many different sewing machines,

Sewing Machine Needs

Here is an example list of your basic sewing-machine needs:

- Buttonhole stitches
- Adjustable feet dogs
- Zigzag stitches if working with jean pockets and belt loops
- Embroidery
- Serger

and I must tell you my all-time favorite machine is the Brother PQ1500-S. I call this my "commercial/home sewing machine," and I actually won it in a drawing. This machine is as fast as a commercial machine, and although it only stitches forward and backward, the machine comes with quite a few feet attachments, and other unique attachments can be purchased down the line. But one of the best things is that it can fit on a small table or desktop and it is very quiet.

A serger cuts and sews the seams at the same time, creating the professional seams you see in ready-to-wear (RTW) garments. There are also many brands and styles to choose from. You can get by with a basic level serger to start, but you really need this machine for your sewing to look professional.

Coverstitch Machine

If you plan on sewing or designing anything with stretch knits, you will need a coverstitch machine. This machine sews the professional-looking hems found in RTW stretch T-shirts, activewear, and knit garments. The coverstitch is sometimes combined in one serger, but I found it very time consuming to keep switching back and forth from coverstitch to serger. Many of the sewing machine companies sell some version of a coverstitch machine. They vary in cost from a few hundred dollars to thousands, depending on your particular needs.

Blind-Stitch Machine

If you are planning on doing alterations, a blind-stitch machine is worth the money. This machine sews only hems, the kind of hem found in nice dress slacks. For years I would hem pants by hand. When I finally forked out the money to buy a blind-stitch machine, it paid for itself in less than one month. Instead of taking thirty minutes to hem a pair of pants, it took less than ten, not to mention that the hems looked more professional. I found my blind-stitch machine at SewTrue.com for under $300 and I have been using the same machine for over eight years.

Pressing Basics

Pressing is the most important aspect of sewing. Believe it or not, pressing makes the difference between a final garment looking professional or home sewn. It is so important to have with the correct tools.

Iron

I have been using a Rowenta Professional iron since I began my business. What I like about this particular iron is that it runs around $100, it does not leak, it doesn't have an automatic shutoff, it has great steam, and it is lightweight. Granted this is not a commercial iron, and I go through one about every year, but the iron is reliable.

Be wary of the inexpensive irons: Many times they drip when steaming and can ruin an entire garment. I ruined $120 worth of fabric when an old, cheap iron had a water moment. I was never able to get all the water spots out!

There are also commercial irons such as gravity feed, steam electric, and mini boilers. If you decide to go with a commercial version, I suggest calling Banasch's (see

Iron Checklist

Here are the three most important things to look for when purchasing an iron:

- ❑ It does not leak.
- ❑ It produces steady steam.
- ❑ Preferably there's no automatic shutoff (because you could spend half your time waiting for the iron to reheat).

appendix); they have a knowledgeable staff and can walk you through which iron will work for what you need. If you decide to purchase a commercial version, make sure you check if you need a special receptacle for power.

Ironing Board or Table

See if you can find an ironing board that is larger than the standard. They are more stable and can fit whole pattern pieces when constructing clothing. You will want to change the standard acrylic ironing board cover to 100 percent cotton; if you cannot find a cotton cover, make one out of basic muslin fabric.

Recently, I converted a six-by-three-foot table into a pressing area. I added a layer of thick, heat-resistant foam and then covered the entire table with muslin. This works great for pressing interfacing to many pattern pieces at once.

Steamer

A professional steamer is not absolutely necessary to start, but you will want to add this when the budget allows. I used a handheld steamer for years, but do be careful of water spotting. Here are some important pressing accessories to consider:

- Sleeve board—narrow board used for pressing sleeves, pant leg seams, or narrow openings
- Ham—instrumental in pressing curves such as collars and princess seams
- Clapper—piece of wood that works with steamed fabric to create creases
- Press cloth—protects fabric while pressing

Dress Form

When working on your garments, whether it is for a custom client or a ready-to-wear line, you will find it very beneficial to have a dress form. When I first started out, I used an adjustable dress form by Dritz. Although this dress form is nice because you can adjust the size, the downside is that it is a little lightweight and tips over very easily. I found this really annoying, and so did my cat; he was the one usually below the tumble. Eventually I used large beanbags at the base to keep the dress form upright. The shell of the Dritz form does not have a lot of padding, which is challenging if you are trying to drape, but for the price, you can make it work.

Eventually, I purchased professional industry-style dress forms. I bought two: One is size 6 and one, size 12, which allowed me to fit many of my clients and work on a ready-to-wear line. You can usually find a base style for under $300, although it is well worth the extra money to add collapsible shoulders and casters at the base. The casters allow you to easily maneuver around the dress form, and the collapsible shoulders are needed for pulling over fitted garments. I have successfully used these dress forms for over ten years, and they have held up perfectly; they are heavy duty and perfect for draping.

Here are some resources for finding professional industry dress forms:

- PGM Dress Forms (www.pgmdressforms.com)
- Dress Rite Forms (www.dressriteforms.com)
- Wolf Form Company Inc. (www.wolfform.com)

Cutting Layout and Tools

When I first started, I purchased a portable cutting table. The problem was the table was not large enough to cut an entire dress or even an entire jacket. For the longer patterns I used my living room floor as a cutting area. Not so great on the knees, but the large space worked great, and I could lay out many pattern pieces together all at once.

Since moving to a larger studio, I purchased multiple waist-high tables from a store that was going out of business. I arranged the tables next to each other, creating a twenty-foot-long and sixty-inch-wide cutting area. I taped numerous standard-size rotary cutting mats to the surface, and now I have the perfect cutting

Expert Tip

Before investing in an expensive cutting table, keep an eye out for retail stores going out of business, and check their supply of display tables.

and pattern-making table. With this layout I can cut with rotary cutters or scissors. Depending on how much space you have, this is the most efficient option If you plan on designing and sewing your own collection.

A rotary cutter and blades can be found at Wawak.com and other sewing supply stores. Although they sell rotary blade sharpeners, save your money and time and just buy new blades. I speak from experience on that one!

Kai scissors are my all-time favorite scissors—the sharpest by far—and can be found at KaiScissors.com. But no matter what brand scissors you buy for cutting fabric, make sure they are sharp, and only use them on fabric. If you use the scissors for other office jobs, the blades become dull quite quickly.

Fitting Area

If you are planning on having clients come to your home, you will need an appropriate fitting area. The area needs to be easily accessible and private so your client can feel comfortable changing clothes. Keep in mind the fitting area will leave a major impression on the client whether you are creating a custom gown or making a simple alteration.

When I first started out I had the clients change in a small half bathroom on the main level. This really did not work so well. The larger-size clients were very uncomfortable and had a hard time changing their clothes in such a small area. There was not enough room to hang their clothes anywhere, and the client had to sit on the toilet seat while putting on her shoes. It did not take long to realize this was not going to work, so I found a three-panel room divider. Clients changed behind it, and as a bonus the front side was all mirrors, which served as a three-way mirror at the same time.

Expert Tip

Build your own dressing area and three-way mirror in one: With supplies from your local home improvement store, hinge together three door panels and attach wall mirrors to each panel on one side or both sides. Very easy and not too expensive!

Mirrors

You need a mirror wide enough for your clients to see themselves and at the same time wide enough for you to see around the client as you pin or alter the garment. I will save you the time—standard wall mirrors are not wide enough. Here are a few alternative ideas:

- Buy three or four of the larger standard mirrors and hang them on the wall next to each other. Make sure you purchase the mirrors without a plastic edge so your mirror will have the appearance of being wider without white or black separating lines.
- Have a mirror cut to fit along a wall or in a certain fitting area, I did this in a condo I was renting. I had a mirror cut seven feet tall and five feet wide to fit in my entrance hallway. The mirror was not fancy—no beveled edges, just a plain old mirror that a glass company installed for me. This mirror has made four moves and still is the main mirror I use in my studio.
- Utilize an existing wall of mirrors. Notice I said an "existing wall of mirrors." When I bought my first house I had an entire wall mirrored, which was rather expensive. The positive was that this made my living room look larger *and* made a great fitting mirror. The negatives of this route were the expense and that those mirrors stayed with the house when I moved.
- Build your own three-way mirror with door panels as mentioned in the "Expert Tip" on page 77.
- Keep an eye out for any retail stores going out of business; many times they will sell off their store fixtures for cents on the dollar.

Lighting

Fluorescent lights can cause colors to appear differently than in the natural light outside; therefore, natural lighting is ideal. If you are fortunate enough to work in an area

Expert Tip

Natural light is very important when deciphering accurate colors, especially when matching thread and fabric.

with windows, take advantage of this and do not cover them up with dark blinds. Another tip is to use "natural light" lightbulbs in your lamps. This is very important when matching fabrics colors and accessories for your clients.

Make sure you have adequate lighting in the fitting and sewing areas. I use the floor lamps with multiple, adjustable bending lamp heads. Retailers like Target usually have these available in many colors for under twenty dollars. Just try sewing black fabric in a dimly lit room for a few hours, and you will know what I mean about having lots of light.

Appearance

When working out of your home, it can be challenging to create a professional image. Creating an exquisite fitting area can help to improve this, so keep in mind that the appearance of your fitting area speaks volumes about your work and your business. Make sure the area is clean, well lit, and private . . . in that order. If your fitting area is cluttered, dusty, and unkept, your client will wonder if they want to leave their clothes with you at all. This holds true whether your business is in your home or in a professional studio—appearance is everything!

Privacy

The dressing area needs to be private. Do not have the client changing in the middle of your living room with your children wandering around. At one point, I used my office as a fitting area. I had to make sure my desk was organized, and I avoided

Fitting Area Checklist

Here is a list of the most important things to consider for your fitting area:

- ❑ Adequate lighting
- ❑ A chair
- ❑ Clean and uncluttered
- ❑ Hooks or a rack to hang clothing
- ❑ Privacy

leaving important paperwork in sight, but this worked out pretty well. Although this was a smaller room, it had the appropriate lighting, a comfortable chair, and allowed a flexible privacy comfort level for the client to shut the door or not.

Office Essentials

While compiling your office equipment, you do not need to spend a lot of money. In fact, with today's technological advancements you can run a fairly good-size business on your own with a good computer system and a few other gadgets. Just remember, most of this equipment is only as good as the user.

Telephone and Voice Mail

If you live alone, you can easily use your existing house phone at first. Just make sure you leave a professional message for callers and always answer the phone as a business. If you have others living with you, add a separate business line. How others might answer the phone is just too chancy, not to mention the risk of missing messages.

So why bother with a business line? Besides the benefit of writing off a business phone on your taxes, is the simple fact that you can list your business in the yellow pages. There are a few options to consider when setting up your business phone. Your current setup will determine which method is best for you.

Adding a Business Phone Line in Your Home

- Phone company—Service is provided through your local phone company. There will probably be an installation fee, but if you also need high-speed Internet this is the route to go because you can install both at the same time.
- Vonage—This reasonably priced Internet-based phone service includes a fax line and visual voice mail. No installation is required, and you can bring the device with you when traveling or if you move. This option does require high-speed Internet.
- Cell phone—This can be a perfectly acceptable option as long as you have an appropriate voice-mail message and do not need a fax line. Just make sure you answer your calls in a professional manner.
- Voice mail—In trying to create a professional image, having a professional business recording on your answering machine is very important.

Here is an example of a professional message: "You have reached ABO Apparel and Fashion Design Studio of Angela Wolf. We are either with a client or away from our desks at this time, so please leave your name, phone number, and a brief message, and we will return your call as soon as possible. Be sure to check out our website, www.AngelaWolf.com, for additional information."

- Visual voice mail—Today's technology offers "visual voice mail" options where messages left on your voice mail can be written out and sent to you via text message. I highly recommend adding this to your plan, as it saves so much time. The busier you get with your business, the more important it is to consolidate your workload. Anything that saves you time while upholding your business standards is ultimately in your favor.

- Toll-free numbers—As your business grows, you might consider adding a toll-free number to your existing phone line, but there really is no need at first. There is usually a minimal fee for this additional service on your existing phone service.

Fax, Scanner, Printer, and Copier

Although faxing seems a thing of the past, there are many times when the fax machine is still needed. Buying an all-in-one printer with a scanner, copier, and fax machine is an inexpensive way to incorporate all of these technology needs into one purchase. For under one hundred dollars you can find a printer/scanner/copier/fax at places like Sam's Club or Costco, which are great resources for computer equipment and office supplies. Their membership fees include a warranty for many of the devices as well.

When you are first starting out there really is no need to have a separate fax line. Vonage, however, offers a free fax line with their business plans, so if you go that route you might as well take advantage. There is also e fax, an Internet-based fax service where you utilize your e-mail account to send and receive faxes.

Computer and Software

A computer is an absolute necessity when going into business for yourself. From keeping tabs on sales to maintaining a working website, a computer can save you time and money. If you already have a basic computer, there is no need to purchase another one to start out. As your business grows you will get a better idea of your computer and software needs. When the time comes to purchase a new computer there are a few things to take into consideration:

- Will you be doing video editing, for example, editing fashion-show videos in order to create marketing tools? Then you will need a computer with a fast processor, large memory capacity, and a separate hard drive. You will also need software such as Pinnacle Studio, Avid, and Movie Maker.
- Will you be doing a lot of photo editing, for example, editing fashion photos for your website, blog, and marketing? Then you will need a computer that comes with a large memory capacity and possibly a separate hard drive. You will also need software such as Photoshop or CorelDraw.
- Will you be doing your own marketing and PR? You will need to consider software such as Publisher, Illustrator, or a similar program.
- What program will you use to maintain your books? You will need to consider software such as Excel, QuickBooks, or Quicken.
- Will you be purchasing a CAD pattern-making system? If this is the case, then you will need a computer with a fast processor and large memory capacity. You will also need software such as Illustrator or CorelDraw that can work with vector drawings and DXF files.
- Do you want your computer to be portable? Consider a laptop or a tablet depending on your needs. Be sure to thoroughly research the features of each and your needs before making a decision.

These lists are just the tip of the iceberg, but it is so much better to ask yourself these questions before buying a new computer in order to make sure your equipment works for you.

Internet

High-speed Internet is readily available and important in order to stay on top of your business. There are many options available, including transforming your smartphone into an Internet connection. Factors such as where you live, how much you travel, and your budget will help determine the option that works for you.

The most common Internet connections are listed below. Keep in mind, technological advancements can cause this list to expand or change at any time.

- Dial-up—through your phone line; economical but slow
- DSL—through your phone line; high speed and much faster than dial-up
- U-verse—through your phone line; higher speed than DSL
- Cable—through your cable line; high speed and even faster than DSL
- Satellite—through a separate satellite outside your home. It is an option if you live in an area where you cannot receive Internet any other way. I found this Internet connection to be rather slow, however.
- Wireless hotspots—through a wireless router. Larger cities are offering areas of free wireless Internet, and the number of locations continues to expand. If you are really on a budget, you can always access the free Internet at a local coffee shop. Just be cautious with an unsecured connection.
- Smartphone data connections—through your cell phone. I use this option when traveling. The speeds are faster than you would think, and the additional fee for data usage is very reasonable. Depending on the particular phone you are using, your smartphone can be used as a wireless hotspot for your computer or tablet to connect to.
- Aircard and mobile hotspots—available through your cell phone company; great for travel, though the smartphone data connection listed above is a less expensive option and equally as fast.

Website

In this day and age, a website is mandatory in business. In fact, I recently read in the *Wall Street Journal* that one of the top ten reasons a business fails is because they do not have a working website. You can always hire someone to do this for you, but this can cost hundreds of dollars. Even if you are a bit technically challenged, there are multiple software options that can walk you through creating your own website in a few hours. Most of the software programs come with basic website templates, and you just have to fill in your personal information. A basic website page should include your logo, a few pictures, and contact information, including your name, business address, phone number, and e-mail address. I have experimented with a few different software packages and found these four to be the easiest and most cost-effective:

- WebEasy—At this time they are up to version 9. The software is very easy to install and set up, and the price is very reasonable. Available at Avanquest.com.

- GoDaddy.com—Offers prebuilt websites that you can put together in a very minimal amount of time. They also host WordPress websites, something to keep in mind if you want to combine your blog and website into one.

- WordPress.com—Mostly viewed as a blogging site, WordPress now offers ways to transform the image of your blog into a professional working website. They have easy tutorials to follow in order to set up. Because your website is saved on the WordPress site, you will not fill up your hard drive, and you can access your website from any computer with your username and password.

- WebPlus—WebPlus offers more features than WebEasy and is a better option if you are looking for an advanced web design template. Available at Serif.com/WebPlus.

A website is essential in establishing a professional image and getting your business information out there. See chapter 9 for more details.

Domain Name

You will need to find an original domain name for your website. The easiest way to accomplish this is to go to GoDaddy.com and see if the name you want is available. If it is, you will be able to purchase the domain name on an annual basis for a minimal fee.

If the domain name you want for your business is not available, check back often in case it becomes available. There is a minimal annual fee in order to continue to hold onto a domain name, so if you are lucky, maybe the current owner will not renew. That is exactly what happened with the domain name I wanted, AngelaWolf .com. For two years the site was unavailable; someone by the name of Angela Wolf had the site with wedding pictures and a wedding announcement. I checked back

Choosing a Domain Name

Things to keep in mind when choosing a domain name:

- Keep the name simple and easy to remember.

- If your business name is long, consider using abbreviations.

- Try to get a "dot-com" (.com) address.

once a month until the site was available again. This is also important to know if you think of skipping out on the minimal fee associated with holding your domain name on an annual basis.

Hosting

After your website is ready to launch you will need to find a company to host your site. Again, GoDaddy.com has inexpensive hosting plans, along with other options, such as site stats, for you to add. There is usually a monthly fee in order to host your site, but this should be minimal. Depending on the software you used to create your site, often times the same software company will offer hosting and even include a few months free.

E-mail Accounts

Consider having separate e-mail addresses in order to keep your business e-mails organized and simplify the daunting task of weeding through e-mails where a large percentage may be junk or advertisements. First of all, it is a good idea to set up an e-mail address linked to your website, which is something you can set up with your hosting company. For example, info@angelawolf.com and pr@angelawolf.com are two separate e-mails linked to my website, AngelaWolf.com. I know the e-mails coming into those two accounts are strictly business related. I also have a personal e-mail that I only give to current clients and friends.

You might consider having a separate e-mail account that you use for everything else: all of the forms you need to fill out on the web, registering products you purchase, e-mail lists you sign up for, newsletters—anything on the web where your e-mail address can be sold to others. I have one e-mail account I use for all of these, and this really cuts down on having to sort through hundreds of e-mails to get to the important messages.

Expert Tip

GoDaddy.com is the best resource out there for help with creating a web presence. If that is not enough, their customer service is unbelievable!

Separating Business from Your Personal Life

When working out of your home, separating business from your personal life is very challenging to say the least. Your current living situation determines which solutions can help with this dilemma.

Living Alone

I lived alone for the first eight years of my business, and I had absolutely no problem allowing the business to take over my entire house. From condo living to a small house, I was totally incapable of separating work from my personal life. My work was my life. If I was home, I was working. In fact, the way I rearranged my home would probably not excite too many people:

- The kitchen: Cooking is not my forte, so I found that kitchen cabinets and pantries created the perfect built-in shelving for fabric.
- The master bedroom: This was by far the largest bedroom and the best area for the sewing and fitting room. I added closet organizers in order to hold excess fabric and sewing supplies. Great lighting and a full-length mirror also created a fitting area.
- Medium bedroom: This was the perfect office and changing area for clients.
- Small bedroom: This was used as my bedroom and closet.
- Finished basement: I found this to be a great cutting area with additional storage space.

This setup worked for many years, but only because I lived by myself. In fact, there were several times I thought I should move my studio out of the house because I needed some space for myself. Well, that did not happen—and then I

Jillian Lewis's Studio in New York

I had the pleasure of visiting Jillian Lewis, a 2008 *Project Runway* contestant, at her home studio in New York. I cannot tell you how thrilled I was to see how similar her condo resembled my house—all fashion, all sewing, all work. The living room and dining room catered to her sewing, sketches, and garment samples. I loved it!

got married. I even talked my husband into moving into my house/business. It did not take long for me to realize this layout was not going to work with two of us in the house.

Married

I continued to run my business out of the house after we got married, but I changed things around a little; for example, I only allowed clients to come by at certain times so as not to interrupt our dinner or evening. I condensed the business to three rooms in the house and filled the kitchen cabinets with dishes. But the most challenging part was still trying to separate my work from our personal life. I would work all day, have dinner with my husband, and head back to the workroom. When I look back, the solution seems so easy. Why on earth did I not create a schedule? When you work for someone else, you work select hours and go home. Of course that is easier said than done.

For the sanity of your marriage and your own self, you need to cut off work at a certain time. Be respectful of your spouse's space in the house and try to prevent your business from overflowing into all aspects of your home environment. Even if you have to schedule it, make quality time for each other.

Expert Tip

Schedule your time wisely and include space for your family!

Weekday Schedule for Custom Apparel:

7:00–10:00	Sewing/designing: no clients
10:00–10:15	Break
10:15–12:30	Client appointments
12:30–1:00	Lunch
1:00–4:00	General business and sewing/client fittings
4:00–6:00	Return e-mails, billing, marketing, ordering fabric and supplies, and other business-related activities
6:00–9:00	NO WORK!
9:00–10:00	Scan Internet and magazines for fashion inspiration

The Last Straw

My husband has always been one of my biggest supporters, but there came a time when even he had to draw the line in the sand and say enough is enough. This day arrived during our second year of marriage. My husband hurt his back at work, so about two o'clock in the afternoon he decided to go home and sit in the hot tub. I was out running errands and did not have any clients for the remainder of the day—or so I thought. Well, one lady had other ideas and just stopped by without an appointment. She rang the doorbell, but no one answered. Seeing the vehicle in the driveway, she walked to the back yard to see if she could find me and instead she found my husband in the hot tub. She proceeded to pull up a chair and visit with him wanting to wait until I made it home. Needless to say, that was the last straw. We moved shortly thereafter, and I made the corporate decision to move the business out the house.

Married with Children

Many people choose to work from home in order to raise their children. There is nothing wrong with this thinking, just be pragmatic about the time you can commit to your new business. Your family will require much of your time, so make sure you are realistic about your goals on your business plan. Maybe you will build your business slowly and work toward creating a strong base for your business until the children are out of the house.

Is Your Home Ready for Clients?

Here is the million dollar question: What does your home really look like? You need to be honest with regard to what you see. Invite a friend over and get their opinion as well. Trust me, they will notice things you might have glanced right over.

Appearance

The appearance of your home is much more than bricks and a driveway. There are three main areas you should focus on: outside appearance, overall cleanliness, and clutter control. All three of these will leave lasting impressions on your clients, especially if they are less than adequate. Even though you are doing business out of your home, you need to take special care to keep a professional environment.

The exterior would be an easy category to overlook, but very important when we talk about first impressions. Is your house inviting or does it look like part of a junkyard with old beat-up cars and "stuff" all over the place? Of course, there are some things you cannot do anything about, but cosmetically you can keep the basics in order. A well-maintained lawn, trimmed bushes, and random flowerpots are nice touches. If you are in the middle of the winter season, shovel the driveway and sidewalk up to your door, which, by the way, was my *least* favorite part of working from home while living in Michigan. Speaking of shoveling, make sure you have special business insurance in place; if a client slips and falls on your property, the liability would fall in your hands, and this will protect you. This is covered in the next chapter.

Pets and Smoking

Animals

You would be surprised to find out how many people are allergic to cats and dogs, including myself. I am not suggesting you get rid of your animals—just take note if someone is allergic and do your best to prevent aggravating their condition.

Most of my clients enjoyed my cat; in fact, he used to sit on the stairs during fittings and pass the pincushion over. One of my clients was so allergic to cats that I offered to go to her house for fittings. If I had any cat hair on my sweater, she would start sneezing uncontrollably. I made a conscious effort to change clothes before visiting her, and on top of that, I made sure her clothes stayed far from my cat while I was sewing them.

Other things to keep in mind if you have pets:

- Pet odors of any kind may be cause for you to lose clients. Keep all kitty litter boxes, birdcages, and the like clean. Consider investing in a continuous-release air freshener to ensure a pleasant environment for clients.
- Keep large dogs in a room or in the backyard. Even small and medium dogs may frighten clients, so be sure to keep Fido in a safe place for his own safety and the safety of your clients.

True Story

I owned one indoor cat, but somehow acquired two additional outdoor kitties, which we named Curly and Moe. These two slept in my garage and became the friendly neighborhood cats. During the summer months, Curly and Moe would leave special gifts at my front door, such as dead mice and chipmunk heads. One morning, I was startled to hear a bloodcurdling scream from outside my home. I opened the front door to find my client screaming and pointing at the half-eaten mouse carcass on my doorstep. Oh, boy! Not exactly the image you want to portray, but sometimes things are out of your hands and you have to make the best of it. From that time forward, I did an early morning "gift" check before my clients would arrive.

Smoking

All you have to do is ask someone who does not smoke and they will confirm that the odor of stale cigarette smoke can be nauseating. If you are the one smoking, you won't be able to detect this smell, so there are a couple of things to take into consideration:

1. Turn your house into a smoke-free environment and take your cigarette breaks outside or in the garage. You would have to do this anyway if you worked in a professional building.
2. If you have been smoking, consider changing your clothes, brushing your teeth, and washing your hands before you see clients. This sounds ridiculous,

but it is true that that smell can linger, and you do not want your clients to think they are leaving their clothes In a dirty, smoke-filled environment.

3. Do NOT smoke in your car while dropping clothes off to a client. Their clothes will pick up the odor, and you will most definitely lose the nonsmoking client.

4. Clean up random cigarette butts from your yard and driveway. I always wonder when I see people throw out their cigarette butts—who do they think is going to clean them up?

Your Space Is Ready!

Let's double check that you have your major essentials in line:

- Sewing equipment and supplies
- Pressing essentials
- Cutting supplies
- Office essentials
- Fitting area
- Website
- Clean house

Now it is time to move into the more technical aspect of your business. Even if you are going to work out of your home, laying out a business plan and making sure you have the legalities in line is very important. Although this chore will be a little mundane, try to add some creative humor to it.

05 Turning Your Fashion Dream into a Business

> Always consider you are opening a business—a fashion business, but still a business and one needs business skills equal to your design skills.
> —*Marsha Brenner, Executive Director of the Apparel Industry Board Inc.*

I know, I can hear the sigh of your yawn right now. Most of us with a creative mind dread the business side. I even went to college to study business, and I still sigh when I have to focus on parts of the business aspect. But one of the biggest failings for fashion designers, especially self-employed fashion designers, is not keeping a business mind about all of your decisions. Creating a business plan, laying out a marketing plan, and staying atop of your finances, just to name a few, are vital. Keeping abreast of the business side of your fashion dream can prevent your dream from quickly become your worst nightmare.

What Is a Business Plan?

For those of us on the creative side, taking the time to sit and write out a formal business plan can be painful, yet from the beginning it is important to form a strategy of how you want your business to run and ultimately a plan for success. Not only will this plan guide you in your business, but it can be used in acquiring financing or securing funds to help in your growth. Unfortunately, many entrepreneurs do not start with a plan, and therefore when they fall into trouble or need guidance, there is nothing to fall back on.

Think of your business plan as a résumé. This document will not only encompass your vision for your business, but this is the nuts and bolts of how your business will run.

Where Do You Want to Be in Two Years?

When you are first getting started it might be hard to envision yourself and your business a few years down the line, but you need to have goals. So where do you foresee your business in two years? Try to be as realistic as possible. You will need to answer this question and resort back to your answers many times in the future. Trust me, once you get started with your business, you will be so busy focusing on the day-to-day workload that you might sway from your true vision and desires without even realizing it.

When I added alterations to my workload, I did not realize how much time that particular business would require. I'm not saying that is a bad thing, but a few years passed before I even realized that my focus had narrowed to alterations and my clothing line was being pushed further and further down the line. If I had kept an eye on my business plan and vision, this would not have happened.

Begin brainstorming on your two-year goals. Close your eyes and picture yourself two years down the line. Here are some suggestions to get you started:

1. I will create one collection (fall/winter) a year for the first two years in order to become acclimated with the process and work out any kinks.
2. I will build a high-end custom apparel clientele with the goal of designing thirty custom gowns within the next two years.
3. I will schedule a "wine and fashion party" one evening a week in order to build my clientele, showcase my expertise, and generate consistent cash flow (see page 37).
4. My clothing line will be sold on my website and in at least six boutiques within the United States.

Once you have your list, go back and add suggestions about how you plan to achieve each goal. For example:

1. Hold an informal fashion show in order to get my name out there.
2. Design a gown pro bono for a friend that will be attending a major gala event.
3. Start a social media campaign around a couture gown I am working on.

See how easy that was? You have now given your business a two-year game plan for success.

Where Do You Want to Be in Five Years?

The five-year goals might be a little more challenging to foresee, but this is your dream. What do you want? Where do you want to be? Here are a few ideas to get you thinking.

1. I will have been designing a fall and spring collection consistently for at least three years now.
2. My clothing will be available on my website as well as in thirty boutiques.
3. I will not need the extra income from alterations, so by the end of five years I will only focus on expanding my clothing line.

Which Market Niche Will You Choose?

Through time you might be designing within a few markets, but why not start with one or two in order to stay focused and not spread yourself too thin. Here are some of the main general options to choose from:

- Women's day apparel
- Women's evening apparel
- Women's plus-size apparel
- Men's day apparel
- Men's evening apparel
- Lingerie
- Teenage apparel
- Knitwear
- Sportswear
- Outerwear
- Bridal
- Maternity
- Kid's apparel
- Baby clothes
- Accessories

Getting the Legalities in Line

Setting up a professional business is really not that difficult, and with only a few hours on the Internet you will have most of the process completed.

Business Identity

What are you going to call your business? Put some thought into your legal business name because this is not something you go changing every year. Think how the name will look on paper and about a possible logo. Make sure the name is easy to pronounce and does not contain profanity or anything that can confuse you with any other company.

It is highly recommended that you do not use your own name for the business name. If the company were to file bankruptcy or has legal issues down the road, you will have a hard time getting your own identity back. That does not mean you cannot use your own name for your clothing label. For example, my legal business name is ABO Apparel, LLC. The ABO is an abbreviation from my first clothing label: Angela Boyer Originals. Thankfully I abbreviated the name, because my married name is different and I would have had to change everything. Underneath the umbrella of ABO Apparel, LLC, I have two clothing labels, Angela Wolf and Angela Wolf Couture, along with a pattern collection that I sell to the home sewer.

DBA

You will need to register your legal name by filing for a fictitious name or DBA (Doing Business As) if you are not using your real name for your business. Check the US Small

Let SBA Help You

SBA.gov has all the information and applications you need about the following:

- Registering your business name (DBA)
- Determining you legal structure
- Employer Identification Number (EIN)
- Sales tax ID number
- Business license and permits
- Trademark
- Copyright

Business Administration website (www.sba.gov) to make sure your business name is available and learn other requirements for your local area.

Business License
Every state and local municipality has different laws and regulations regarding small businesses. Please research your area carefully to ensure that you have all the legal paperwork required. Registering your business at your local city level is required and usually has a minimal fee.

Business Structure
In choosing your business structure, take into consideration the size of your business. When I first started out I ran my business as a sole proprietorship. I later changed to an LLC in order to separate my name with the business name. Each identity has different fees and tax implications, so if you are unsure of which one to choose, consult with your accountant.

- Sole Proprietors (business owned by one person)
- Partnerships (business owned by two or more people)
- Corporation (separate legal identities from the person who started the business: limited liability company, or LLC; S-Corporation; C-Corporation)

Trademark
A trademark is a word, name, symbol, letter, or something that distinguishes a certain business or product from others. Once you have a logo or name, it is not mandatory to apply for a trademark, but it's simply a good idea to protect your product image. A registered trademark also allows you to place the symbol ® alongside your protected name or logo.

The United States Patent and Trademark Office (www.uspto.gov) has information on applying for a trademark. The current base fee associated with applying for a trademark yourself is $325, and if you go through an attorney the cost might double. There is more to come on trademarks in chapter 8.

Sales Tax ID
A sales tax ID or resale license is needed in order to sell your products. It is a requirement for you to collect sales taxes on what you are selling, and in return, the sales tax

you collect is then paid to the state on an annual, quarterly, or monthly basis. Take note: If someone from another state orders an outfit from you, you are not required to collect sales tax on that garment. There has been a lot of push for the government to change that law as well as states that do not charge sales tax, so make sure you check the current laws in your state.

Wholesalers require you to have a sales tax number before they will sell you fabric and supplies. You will purchase their materials without paying taxes immediately. Instead you will charge sales tax to your client on your finished product and then pay the state. Be sure to keep good records of anything that you purchase that you owe taxes on. There is also a "use tax" that you will need to pay if you keep any of the supplies or fabrics for your own personal use.

In order to apply for a resale license do an Internet search for "Board of Equalization" in your local state for an application. There is usually not a charge for this license, but every state is different.

Federal EIN

Think of an EIN number as your business' social security number. When you first start your business you can use your own social security number, but because of identity theft, I strongly urge you to apply for an EIN number right away. This license is free of charge and you can apply online at IRS.gov, and in minutes you will have your own number.

Thinking into the future, it is required for a business to have an EIN number if you have employees or hire contractors. But what you might not realize is that if you order wholesale fabric from a mill overseas, they will also require an EIN number. It's free, easy, and fast, so just get it done.

Banking

Setting up a business checking account is very simple, but it is important to comparison shop the banks for fees and requirements. Make a few phone calls and ask the following:

1. Do they have free business checking?
2. What is the minimum amount required to open the account?
3. Does the account pay interest?
4. Do they charge per check written and/or deposit made into that account?

You need to bring your DBA or articles of corporation paperwork, along with your minimum deposit to get started. Sometimes banks give free checks when you first sign up, but if not take a look at ChecksUnlimited.com or Walmart.com for good deals.

Insurance

You will need to purchase additional insurance to cover your business equipment and supplies, along with additional liability if you are planning on having clients visit your home. With the additional coverage for your business equipment, you will want to itemize your machines and list additional inventory. This will help protect your investment in case of fire or theft. Check with your insurance agent and explain what you do; they will be able to identify your exact policy needs.

An umbrella policy adds extra coverage beyond your auto and homeowner's insurance coverage, so you would purchase this in addition to your current policies. It is highly recommended that you have at least a $1 million umbrella policy. Even if you do not have a million in assets, if you are ever sued, you could be required to pay out based on your current assets and future earnings. Another factor that surprised me: If I am ever sued, the umbrella policy will help to cover legal fees, even if I win the court case. The cost to add an umbrella policy varies, but in general it's about $200 a year, in addition to your current policy. When just starting your business, you might be tight on cash flow, so you can always raise your deductibles in order to counter the cost.

When you are checking rates for your home insurance, also check for discounts if you use the same company for your homeowner's and vehicle insurance. I have been offered discounts based on several factors:

- Credit score
- Having an alarm system
- Using the same company for home and car insurance
- Being a nonsmoker
- Using OnStar in the vehicle
- My past (good) driving record

Health insurance is another insurance that you will need. Of course, if you have a working spouse who has insurance coverage that covers you, then you are very fortunate. Even if you are young and healthy, an accident or major sickness can happen without warning. One hospitalization without insurance could leave you with tens of thousands of dollars of debt. There are minimal health insurance policies that will at least cover you if you are hospitalized; many of these also cover an annual physical. The deductibles are higher, but if you are fairly healthy then I would take this route. If you have preexisting conditions, then you might look for a better policy that even covers prescriptions. Just make sure you ask questions and explain to your insurance agent that you are starting a new business, and compare the costs with different deductibles and with different coverage. With the insistence of my mother, I bought my first health insurance policy when I was a very healthy twenty-four-year-old. I ended up paying over $300 a month because I did not know to ask for different options. I realized a few years later that I was paying for the best coverage, full prescription coverage, and a very low deductible, all of which I did not need at the time.

Today many of the health insurance companies are more about preventative health than they have been in the past. There are quite a few fitness clubs that offer discounts and waive the initiation fees based on which health insurance company you use. For example, Blue Cross Blue Shield tied in with the national franchise Anytime Fitness offering discounts and incentives. Not only that, once I signed up on their website I began receiving coupons for lots of good stuff. A friend of mine's

Flood Insurance

It is important to ask your insurance agent specific questions on what you will be covered for; there might be additional policies you need to add in order to protect yourself. I learned this the hard way when my basement flooded. I usually stored my fabric off the floor in racks, but within a typical workday a few bolts of fabric would ultimately end up on the floor along with scattered patterns and supplies. One evening we had a terrible rainstorm, and my basement ended up with about an inch of water. Needless to say, the bolts of silk charmeuse and Italian wool that were left on the floor made like a sponge and soaked up all the water. Thousands of dollars of fabric and supplies were completely ruined! I called my insurance agent only to find out that I did *not* have coverage for flooding. In fact, it turned out I did not even have coverage if my sump pump gave out. For only a few dollars more a month, I would have had coverage for my soaking wet fabric—if only I had known what questions to ask!

health insurance company even offered discounts on her health insurance premium if she could prove she went to the gym four days a week. Well, if you are footing the bill, you might as well enjoy the perks.

Create Your Own Successful Business Plan

You want a business plan that tells the story of your business. The plan should answer who, what, when, where, and how this will happen. Your plan should be focused and clear on your particular business goals. Lastly, do not just throw this document in a file; update it often. When your vision changes or your outlook takes a turn, keep your plan up to date. There are many software packages that offer help in writing a business plan, but I have not found one that really incorporated fashion designing. Instead, check out SBA.gov and Business.USA.gov for free tutorials and expert advice—they walk through the entire business plan. I also found that if you search "business plan" on the Internet, there are numerous free formats to follow.

Executive Summary

The executive summary is the most important part of your business plan. It is suggested that you write this part last because it will be the synopsis of your entire business plan. This summary might be the only thing a possible investor or bank will look at, so it needs to be concise and literally describe your entire business in under two pages. Keep this summary enthusiastic about who you are and what you do. Think of it as the hook that could draw someone in to read more of what you have to offer. If your summary is poorly written, it is highly doubtful someone will want to read further about your vision and what you have to offer.

Business Development and Vision

This is the section where you will summarize your mission statement. According to the *World English Dictionary*, a mission statement is "an official statement of the aims and objectives of a business or other organization." Include a brief history of your business along with your particular goals and objectives. You could also include past accomplishments as well as any unique qualifications you might have.

You will also need to estimate you potential business growth. This is a little tricky when you first start out, but as your business grows you will gain a clearer picture into your business potential, and this is exactly why you should continue to update this business plan on a regular basis.

Market Analysis

Do some research into the category of fashion design you are planning on entering, narrowing in on your target market. Create a general profile of the client you are targeting with your merchandise.

Browse other designers, retail stores, boutiques, and online sites, and determine what share of the market you anticipate for your collection. Are you going to stay small and sell in only a select few boutiques or are you going to focus on Internet sales? Maybe you already have a share in the market with your product; now analyze exactly where to expand.

Industry Analysis

Analyze the market size for your product and analyze the industry trends. Is there a need in the fashion industry for your product or service? Are you filling a niche? For example, if you design jeans in the price point of $300 retail, what makes your jeans different? What will make a client choose you over another designer? It could be the quality of fabrics and construction, or the fact that you offer a service such as custom sizing. Analyze the market and see if there is a gap that you can fill with your product.

Customer Analysis

Now ask yourself, who is your customer? Create a list of your customer demographics, starting with the following:

- Gender
- Age
- Income
- Location
- Lifestyle

Try to analyze what your customers are all about. Do they prefer quality and service or price? The deeper you can delve into your ideal client, the better chance you have at offering a product they cannot resist.

Competitive Analysis

A competitive analysis will determine the strengths and weaknesses of other designers you are competing with directly. Research the designers that are similar to your price point and design aesthetic. Where are they selling? Who are they targeting? How are they marketing themselves?

You can easily scan magazines, websites, and online retail stores in order to see how other designers are marketing their brand and selling their products.

Products and Services

Describe the product or service that you are offering in detail. Include the price points of your products and how you plan to be competitive.

Organization and Management

- What is the overall structure of your business: proprietorship, partnership, or corporation?
- List any special licenses or permits that your business will need to operate.
- Include biographies of any key managers involved in the business, including yourself.
- Describe the overall layout of your company, including who will be responsible for what.

Marketing and Sales Strategy

A focused marketing and sales strategy allows you to use your resources wisely in order to attract customers. A marketing plan explains the sales strategy of the following:

- **Products and services** (description of the product or service)
- **Promotions** (develop a marketing plan around your budget)
- **Price** (create a pricing strategy as far as discounts and promo)
- **Place and distribution** (where you will sell your product: retail, website, catalog, custom, etc.)
- **Packaging** (describe customer service that you will provide, for example, custom sizing)

Financial Management

If you are a new business you might not have much to go on immediately in the financial management, but there are a few basics to get you started.

Estimate your start-up costs:

- Equipment
- Supply list

Try to project your income and expenses one year out:

- Projected balance sheet one year out (a glimpse of the company's financial situation and includes: assets, liabilities, and equity)
- Projected income statement one year out (also referred to as the profit and loss or P&L)
- Projected cash flow one year out (the movement of money in and out of the business)

It is important to try to design a budget based on your projected income and expenses. Understandably, when you are first starting out this can be a difficult challenge, but you need to have a base to start with. As your business grows you can adjust the financials accordingly.

A Priceless Resource

Laying out your business plan will really help in keeping your focus. It is a great resource to go back to and expand on as your business grows. Even if you do not write out your business plan in a professional manner, just having something in writing with your vision at this time is a priceless tool in order to stay focused and to be able to grow your business with a strategic plan. As far as some of the legalities you need to have in order, if you find this a challenge it might be wise to hire an attorney or seek other guidance. Remember, there is only so much you can do, and you are the only one who knows what you can accomplish. If there is something outside of your understanding and know-how, hiring a professional will outweigh the costs of possible mistakes and time wasted.

06 | Financial Planning and Management

We're moving on to the financial planning and management of your money that will flow in and out of your business. It is easy to say that you will be generating a steady cash flow consistently week to week, month to month, year to year, and so on, but the reality in the fashion design business is a bit different. Looking at a twelve-month calendar you could spend eight months developing and selling a collection and only four months collecting money. This is really important to understand in order to make the numbers work for your business and to prevent going bankrupt within the first few years. It can be very tempting to lavishly spend money during the few months you generate an income if you do not have a good financial plan in place.

Start-Up Costs

If you are not careful, you can quickly end up over budget when starting your business. From equipment to office supplies, try to keep a strict budget and avoid the impulse purchases. Create a list of the items that are absolutely necessary to get started, including a business license, equipment, insurance, and so on. List the item and the cost. On another sheet add the items that come to mind that can wait for now but which you would like to add in the future. Keep an eye on sales and add these items at a later date. See page 105 for few items to get you started.

Securing Financing

The bottom line is that if you want to sell to more and more retailers, you are going to need access to larger sums of money. After you design a collection and you spend a month taking orders from retail stores, you are responsible for

Start-Up Costs Projection

Item	Initial Cost	Running Total
LLC license	$145	$145
Local city license	$10	$155
Business telephone line	$100	$255
Sewing machine	$640	$895
Iron	$120	$1,015
Dress form	$320	$1,335
Laptop	$450	$1,785
Domain	$13	$1,798
QuickBooks	$229	$2,027
Website software	$39	$2,066
Miscellaneous office supplies	$150	$2,216
Miscellaneous sewing supplies	$200	$2,416
Pattern-making supplies	$120	$2,536

Shopping tip: The day after Thanksgiving is a perfect day to stock up on office and computer items; the prices are unbeatable!

purchasing the fabric and having the apparel manufactured, all of which will need to be paid for before you receive payment for your product.

Getting a Bank Loan

We have watched lending terms change drastically over the last few years. Banks have tightened their belts and now make it a bit challenging for new businesses to borrow money. As your business grows and you can prove financial stability, banks will look much more favorably on loaning you money. Another key ingredient is being able to show projected sales or current orders on hand. My best advice would be to make an appointment with your local banker, bring in your business plan and financial statements, and explain what you are trying to accomplish. You might be able to get a prior financial commitment from your banker for your next collection. Then you can feel secure taking a certain amount of orders and knowing that you will have the funds to fulfill the orders.

Credit Card Use

Using credit cards as a way to run your business can be expensive, but as a new business owner you might not have any other options. It is a good idea to apply for a business credit card in order to establish credit, not to mention a credit card can help when cash flow is tight. Just be careful not to maintain a high balance for a long period of time, if you can help it. The interest rates most credit cards charge are astronomical, and when compounded over time, they can leave you dead in your tracks. Be very prudent with the purchases you make with the credit card and make it a goal to pay off your purchases every thirty or sixty days if possible.

Borrowing from Other Sources

- **Government grants**—In trying to bring manufacturing back to our country and with a demand for apparel made in America, the government seems to be stepping up its funding options. I have recently read of a few different grant options for fashion designers and apparel manufacturers. All of these can change with a snap of a finger, but it is definitely something worth checking into if you need money in order to expand your business. Check out Business.USA.gov and GovernmentGrants.org for resources on SBA loans and government grant options.
- **Home equity loans**—If you own the house you live in and you have considerable equity in it, you could apply for a home equity loan. The interest rates are usually higher than your actual mortgage rate, but less than if you were to use a credit card. One benefit of the home equity loan is that you can write off the interest that you pay each year, but at the same time if you only pay the minimum payment you will always be paying interest and never pay the loan off. Also, keep a close eye on any signing fees or prepayment penalties.
- **Venture capitalist**—A venture capitalist is a person or company that provides capital for new or unproven business adventures. Venture capitalists are usually interested in loaning money to high-risk businesses. When you are first getting started, this probably will not be a viable option for you, but as you continue to grow in your business keep this one in mind. If you have received a substantial amount of orders, you might be able to find a venture capitalist to supply you with money in order to manufacture your apparel.

Pricing to Make a Profit

One of the most challenging aspects of running your own business is pricing your product to make a profit. If you are doing most of the sewing yourself, do not discount your time as nothing. Even if you are not making enough money to give yourself a paycheck at first, you still need to factor in your time when pricing your garments. As your business grows, you may need to hire out some of the work you are currently doing, and this extra cost needs to be figured in to each garment from the beginning. For myself, the most difficult part was figuring what this cost should be. When I first started my business, I was way undercharging for my services. I did not have the confidence to charge what I should have been charging, and I see this as a common denominator with others in this field. This is especially true in the custom apparel and alteration business. When it comes to pricing garments to sell in a boutique, the mathematics can be a little more clear, but there is still a tendency to discount your labor cost.

Before you can begin pricing your product, you need to come up with an hourly rate for yourself. What is the value of your time? Twenty dollars an hour? Sixty dollars an hour? When you first start your business, most of the money you make will probably go right back into your business, but eventually you will have to pay yourself something or your business will not be sustainable. Once you have established a base rate for yourself, double that rate and use this new figure when pricing the labor for your products. If it takes you forty hours to design a gown for a custom client and your base rate is forty dollars an hour, then your labor cost is sixteen hundred dollars. Now keep in mind, that sixteen hundred dollars does not include materials or fixed overhead, not to mention a profit.

Pricing Your Items

Cost of Material + Labor + Fixed Expenses + Profit = Garment Cost

This simple formula incorporates all of your costs into your garment. Before you go and buy bolts of fabric, yards of trim, and hundreds of buttons, take the time to figure the cost of the garment. Will your price be competitive? This is especially true if you are designing a ready-to-wear collection. Can the market bear your retail price point? If your simple T-shirt design is coming in with the wholesale cost of one hundred dollars and you know your buyers will only spend fifty dollars, it is better to know now before you begin purchasing supplies and manufacturing.

Estimate Cost Worksheet for Custom Apparel

Client: _____

Phone:_____E-mail: _____

Addess: _____

Description of Garment:

_____

_____

_____

_____

_____

Materials	Description	Quantity	Cost	Total Cost	Sketch
Fabric					
Lining					
Interfacing					
Underlining					
Thread					
Notions: zippers, buttons, trim, etc.					
Labels & tags					
Packaging					
Extras					
Labor		Hours	Rate	Total Cost	
Sewing					
Fittings					Order Date:
Custom muslin sample pattern out of inexpensive fabric					Completion Date:
Additional shipping costs					

Estimate Cost Sheet for RTW

Style #   Season   Size range
Description:

Front sketch	Back sketch		
Comments:			
Costs:	Quantity	Price	Total Amount
Fabrics:			
Lining:			
Interfacing;			
Underlining:			
Trims:			
Grading:			
Marking:			
Cutting:			
Samples:			
Packaging:			
Labels:			
Total Cost:			
Wholesale price:			
Retail price:			

Factors to Take into Consideration

Cost of Materials

Any materials that go into the garment need to be accounted for. Some of the obvious costs are fabric, trims, buttons, interfacing, and thread. But don't forget about labels, hangtags, garment bags, or hangers. Even if your care labels only cost you ten cents apiece, they still need to be added to your bottom line. I usually keep a checklist of the most common materials I use frequently, along with pricing, so I can easily incorporate this into my garment cost. See the cost sheet examples on pages 108 and 109 for reference.

Labor

If your garment is made in a factory or you have hired a subcontractor, this labor cost has been defined for you. Are you hiring out a pattern maker, grader, or sample maker? All of these costs must be included. If you are doing the designing, cutting, and sewing yourself, factor in the hourly rate you have established for yourself and double it.

Business Overhead

The business overhead includes your fixed expenses—expenses that you will incur regardless whether you sell ten garments or five hundred garments. Some examples of fixed expenses include:

- Rent
- Utilities
- Membership dues
- Magazine subscriptions
- Business phone
- Insurance
- Internet
- Business website
- Annual equipment maintenance

Profit

Adding a profit margin to your product is essential. First of all, there are costs associated with business that you might have missed when figuring your business overhead. Ideally you do not want to have to take this excess cost out of your profit, but at least you have it there to take from. Again, an easy way to price your garments when you first get started is to figure all of the costs that go into the garment, including labor, and double it. This is called *keystoning*, the pricing method of marking merchandise for resell to an amount that is double the wholesale price.

Financial Statements

An income statement, also referred to as a profit and loss statement or P&L, is your business' financial statement. This statement explains how revenue from the sale of your products translates into net income. The purpose of the financial statement is to quickly show if you are making money or losing money during a certain period of time. If you plan on borrowing money from a bank, they will expect to see your financial statements.

Monthly, Quarterly, and Annual Reports

The good news is that software packages like QuickBooks enable you to keep track of your P&Ls with a quick click. As long as you continue to input your revenue and detailed expenses, you will have quick access to your overall financial picture. As you get rolling on your business, it is a good idea to print off monthly P&Ls just as a quick way of keeping tabs on the financial health of your business. You might be selling large quantities of clothing, but if your P&L is showing that you are losing money, the faster you catch it, the faster you can fix it.

Additional Income Options

When you are first getting started in your business, it might be very probable that you will have to have a second job in order to sustain an income. Make sure you do not incorporate this extra income into your business financial statement, unless it pertains to your business. At the same time, if your main business focus is custom apparel and you have added alterations and wardrobe consulting as a way to generate cash flow, you might want to keep this under a separate financial statement or at least make sure this income is itemized correctly.

Contracts

When signing a contract with your client, keep the original in your files and give the client a copy. If for some reason you or the client decide to cross anything out on the original, make sure you both initial any and all changes. A fellow designer friend of mine had a contract with a client and accidentally gave the client the original signed form. Things did not go well with this entire garment, but in the end the client refused to pay the final costs. The client even brought the designer a copy of the original contract with items crossed out, obviously crossed out by the client without the consent of the designer. There is not much you can do in this situation, so be meticulous on finalizing contracts.

Invoicing and Billing

Whether you require payment up front or at the time of delivery, your invoice will be basically the same. Always have your logo, business name and address at the top. Depending on your payment terms, include this on the invoice. If you allow thirty days (net 30), you might consider adding a fee if paid after the thirty days. That might sound trivial, but it can make a difference in how fast you receive your payment. It's just the same as if you offer a discount if paid within ten days. For example, you might offer a 10 percent discount if paid by check within ten days. Just make sure this is clear on the invoice.

Creating a Budget

A budget is a financial plan for saving, borrowing, and spending. The budget you create at the beginning of your business will probably change monthly, but at least have a base to start with. You have a list of your fixed overhead expenses, and you know this amount will go out every month regardless of what you bring in. Now you need to project how much revenue you anticipate bringing in over a select period of time. For example, if you have orders for two custom gowns next month, you know how much money will be coming in. Is this amount enough to cover the expenses that you know need to be paid that same month?

As another example, if you are designing a ready-to-wear collection and you know there will be a six-month period from the time you start the collection to the time that you will be paid for items sold, this needs to be factored into your budget. At first, six months without pay can be very challenging, but as long as you have forecast this you can try to make other arrangements. As time goes by, and you continue to create new collections, when the revenue comes in from your sales you will hopefully be able to maintain a budget for each concurring period.

Do not avoid dealing with your financials. If you are struggling with getting your business off the ground or you are going through a period where your business is

Angela ☆ Wolf

www.AngelaWolf.com

Custom Apparel Contract

Date_____

Customer_____   Pickup Date _____

Total Cost_____   (see attached invoice)

Fittings: It is important to bring any undergarments that you plan on wearing with your garment, including any special bra, body shapers, and nylons. You will also need to bring your shoes and anything else you are adding or wearing to the finished garment. This garment will require _____ fittings.

Payment: A 50% deposit is required at the time of signing. The final 50% is due after we have finished your muslin, before the fabric and trim is ordered. We accept cash, check, debit cards, and all credit cards.

Additional Charges: Any changes to this agreement may result in additional charges. This includes drastic weight change resulting in having to refit the original garment. Changes to the design or fabric and embellishing.

- Please note: there will be a $25 charge for any missed fitting appointments without prior notice.

Returns and Exchanges: As this is a custom garment created special for you and fit to your exact shape there are no refunds or exchanges.

Cancellation: In the event you cancel this agreement at anytime, you will still be responsible for all labor and materials that we have incurred up to the time of cancellation.

Finished Garment: You will be asked to sign a release upon delivery or pickup of your new garment, acknowledging that you have received the garment and that it has been completed to your satisfaction. Any additional changes that you might like after this stage will result in additional charges.

Garment Care: The fabric used in your garment has been pre-cleaned according to the enclosed labels. It is highly advised to follow these directions for future cleanings.

Thank you again for your order, and I look forward to working with you.

Customer Signature _____   Angela Wolf _____

Print Name _____   Date _____

Phone: 269.556.9746   Fax: 269.934.0446   Email: info@angelawolf.com

ABO APPAREL, LLC
185 E. Main St.; Suite 102
Benton Harbor, MI 49022
Toll Free: 866.618.2524

Invoice

Date	Invoice #
6/26/2012	1

Bill To
Jane Doe 4211 Lake Street Chicago, Il 60645

www.AngelaWolf.com

info@angelawolf.com

Description	Amount
Custom Mother of the Bride	3,400.00
Ordered 4/20/2012—To be picked up 6/26/2012	
100% silk dupioni gown with hand-beaded jacket—fully lined with silk charmeuse Dry clean only	
Initial Deposit 4/20/2012 Michigan Sales Tax	-1,700.00 204.00

| **Total** | $1,904.00 |

very slow, you might be tempted to avoid looking at any financials. In order to run a successful business you need to keep tabs on your company's financial status at all times, regardless of what they might reveal.

Building Credit with Vendors

In any business, it takes time to build a relationship with vendors. The best way to build this relationship is to be reliable and consistent in your business practices. Pay your bills on time, especially when it comes to purchasing supplies and working with contractors. If they send you an invoice to pay within thirty days, then do it, even if it's the twenty-ninth day. A good way to stay on top of paying your bills on time is to set up your business bank account with online banking. This will allow you to pay a bill in two minutes, and you won't even have to scrounge for a stamp. If you are not familiar with online banking, you simply log into your bank account and set up a vendor account for each bill that you need to pay. You simply punch in how much you want to pay and the date you want the bill paid and the bank mails the check for you. The vendor receives a professional business check from you, on time.

As you build a reputation with these vendors, they might eventually allow you to have payment terms or extend you credit for a period of time (usually thirty to sixty days), but when you first start out you better plan on paying up front. Set up a business credit card (you can do this through your bank) and consider adding a debit card to your business checking account. I found both of these very useful when working with vendors that require immediate payment. I rarely carry checks with me, especially business checks. When going to trade shows, new vendors will want payment

Cash Is King!

Cash flow is really the key ingredient for any business to maintain and thrive, although creating a consistent cash flow is much easier said than done. By keeping close tabs on your financial position you have a better chance of keeping adequate cash on hand for when it is needed. I have found that many of the vendors I do business with offer a discount if I pay with cash instead of credit cards. Plan for this. There are times when using a credit card is your only option, but when cash is on hand, make sure you use it to your best advantage.

Example of Cash Flow Projection

The chart below is an example of a projected cash flow if you were designing two collections a year. You can see the four months a year you will be generating an income. If you take a look at the fashion design schedule in chapter 1, you can see how the income coincides with the delivering of your clothes to the stores. The stores do not pay until you deliver the goods, so you can see how keeping an eye on your cash flow projection is very important. If you are designing custom apparel, there will probably be a steadier cash flow, but not necessarily. For example, if you focus on wedding gowns and evening wear, you might see an influx of cash during the summer months and the holiday season, yet not much during the off season.

When you first start out this projection will be difficult to predict, therefore you might want to forecast a few months at a time until you get a handle on what you are capable of generating. If you add alterations to the business you can even run off reports with weekly projections as well. With alterations, each week you have finished items, dropped off, picked up, and new work scheduled for the following week. I use QuickBooks, and I can alter the date range for any of my charts and reports.

	Accounts Receivable	Accounts Payable	Net Inflows	Projected Balance
Beginning Balance	8,100.00	0.00		8,100.00
Mar '12	3,400.00	800.00	2,600.00	10,700.00
Apr '12	0.00	1,200.00	-1,200.00	9,500.00
May '12	0.00	2,300.00	-2,300.00	7,200.00
Jun '12	0.00	800.00	-800.00	6,400.00
Jul '12	0.00	820.00	-820.00	5,580.00
Aug '12	8,100.00	0.00	8,100.00	13,680.00
Sept '12	3,400.00	800.00	2,600.00	16,280.00
Oct '12	0.00	3,600.00	-3,600.00	12,680.00
Nov '12	0.00	5,800.00	-5,800.00	6,880.00
Dec '12	0.00	2,000.00	-2,000.00	4,880.00
Jan '13	0.00	2,100.00	-2,100.00	2,780.00
Feb '13	8,400.00	1,200.00	7,200.00	9,980.00
Mar '13	3,600.00	1,400.00	2,200.00	12,180.00
Apr '13	0.00	1,200.00	-1,200.00	10,980.00
May '13	0.00	6,300.00	-6,300.00	4,680.00
Jun '13	0.00	2,200.00	-2,200.00	2,480.00
Jul '13	0.00	2,300.00	-2,300.00	180.00
Aug '13	8,100.00	0.00	8,100.00	8,280.00
Sept '13	4,300.00	0.00	4,300.00	12,580.00
Mar '12–Sept '13	39,300.00	34,820.00	4,480.00	
Ending Balance	47,400.00	34,820.00		12,580.00

up front, so the debit card and credit card are a necessity, and my business name is on both. At the end of each month, I can compare my statements and make sure I recorded all my expenses for the month. Just make sure you grab the right card: With the debit card, money comes out of your bank account immediately, unlike a credit card, which you pay later.

Extending Credit to Clients

Extending credit to your clients really depends whether you are working with clients one on one, such as in custom apparel, or selling your clothing line to retail outlets. When it comes to custom apparel, I highly recommend getting at least a 50 percent nonrefundable deposit at the first consultation. This not only confirms that your client is agreeing to pay for the garment you are designing for her, but it protects you if a client changes her mind because she happened to go on a shopping spree and find a different dress. Once you have finished the final muslin fitting with the client, then you should require full payment, unless you are working with a long-time client. This is to protect you: There is nothing worse than ordering hundreds of yards of fabric to find out that your client has changed her mind on the style of the garment or she simply wants a different color.

If you design wedding gowns or any apparel associated with weddings, I would require a full, nonrefundable payment up front. Without taking into consideration the fickleness of some of the brides, you would be amazed at the number of weddings that are canceled. You do not want to be stuck with a finished custom wedding gown!

When selling to retail outlets, the usual practice is to require full payment before you ship the merchandise to their store. Make sure you have their credit card information on file and charge their card before the items leave your studio.

Getting Organized

Now that you have a handle on the initial start-up costs required to get your business off the ground, and hopefully you have the money in place or at least know where you will access it from, we move into organizing. It is vital to keep a close eye on the financial health of your business from the beginning. As you grow it can be tempting to avoid the finances, especially during the slow times. Then, when you are rolling in the money, you might not see the need to monitor. Put on your business cap and pay attention! In the fashion industry, cash flow is not consistent month to month, so financial planning and budgeting is very important.

The Lavender Bride
FROM LINDA STEWART

Even when you follow all the right steps to protect yourself, you can be taken by a client. The "Lavender Bride" is a perfect example. Several years ago, early in the summer, I was contacted by a bride who wanted a lavender wedding gown. She was very specific. She wanted high-quality silk fabric, real pearls, and Swarovski crystals. I sourced the fabric for over six weeks, finally locating the perfect lavender silk from England. The dress was designed with custom embroidery that took two machines, eight hours a day, for two full weeks to complete.

We agreed on a price of $6,000 plus tax. The contract was approved by my lawyer and was very specific. One-third of the cost was due at the signing of the contract, and it stated exactly what was included in that price. The balance was due when the gown was completed. The contract was signed in October, and a firm date of completion for June 1 the following year was agreed upon.

I received a check for the deposit of $2,000 and the check cleared. I made a copy of the check. In the long run it did no good, because by the time I realized I was not to get the balance due, the account had been closed.

In April of the following year, just six weeks before the completion date, the bride called to tell me the wedding had been canceled. I reminded her that the contract stated if the wedding were canceled she would have the option of having the dress completed or pay me at the rate of fifty dollars per hour for work already completed. She stated she wanted the dress finished, so I moved ahead.

After a scheduling delay on the bride's part, on July 19 the Lavender Bride tried on the dress for the final fitting. All was perfect. Unfortunately she did not have the money to pay the amount due. (I never let a garment leave my studio without payment in full.) She assured me a check would be delivered within the week. She left; I never saw her again. I tried tracking her for four years as she moved across the country. I easily won a judgment against her, but unless there is a way to get to the money (privacy laws make this nearly impossible), a judgment is not much more than a piece of paper.

I finally located her, but before the judge could issue a summons to appear before him, she filed for bankruptcy. My judgment was listed among a long list of judgments against her, and all were literally wiped away by the stroke of another judge's pen.

I have since changed my contract to state that half of the cost is nonrefundable and due upon signing the contract, with the balance due at the time of the first fitting.

I still have the gown; it has appeared in *Threads* magazine and on the runway at the Association of Sewing and Design Professionals conference in Denver. If you know of someone who is looking for a beautiful silk lavender gown, I've got just the gown for you!

Bookkeeping and Taxes

When you are starting a new business the last thing you have is extra time; therefore, you might be tempted to forgo setting up a good, detailed bookkeeping system. I can tell you from experience that it is a lot more efficient in the long run to lay out a computerized format immediately. Not only will this get you started on the right path, but hopefully this will prevent you from picking up bad habits. This chapter walks you through getting organized for business.

Keeping Good Records

Starting your own business is challenging enough, but if you do not keep good records throughout the year you will be pulling your hair out at tax time. Whether you use advanced software or resort to an old-time written ledger, money that comes into the business and money that goes out must be documented and recorded. It is a good idea to lay out your record-keeping plan before you open the doors for business. This does not mean that you cannot change your system down the road, but at least you have a place to start.

Software Options

There are many software programs to choose from in order to assist with bookkeeping and invoicing. I have listed three of the most popular versions, of which I personally use QuickBooks. I have to admit I only use about one-tenth of what the software offers, simply because I have not taken the time to familiarize myself with all of the options. With that being said, the little I do know saves me a ton of time and energy when it comes to keeping track of expenses and inventory, not to mention the efficiency for invoicing and creating estimates. Whichever software package you choose, remember the software is only as good as the user. If you have difficulties configuring the software to your business, you can ask your accountant to set it up for you or keep an eye out for classes in your local community.

- Microsoft Excel
- QuickBooks
- Quicken

Track Income and Expenses

One of the reasons I like QuickBooks is that I literally spent one hour following their tutorial, answering all their questions, and that was it. From that point forward, as long as I have input all my income and expenses correctly, the software will automatically transform that data into usable worksheets and reports. With a click of a mouse I can access a quick overview of my entire business or break it into daily, weekly, monthly, or annual reports.

Filing System

Being a creative person, of course I am going to come up with a unique filing system. I utilize two filing cabinets, one for expenses and invoicing and the other for supplier information, such as catalogs and sale flyers. I use multicolored folders for filing:

- Red—general expenses
- Purple—invoices from any supplier (fabric, trim, fabric dye, etc.)
- Green—receivables and client information

Sample Income/Expense Tracker

Date	Description	Category	Expense	Income	Balance
6/10/2012	Sewing machine attachment	Equipment	$149		$849
6/12/2012	Alterations	Alterations		$325	$1174
6/13/2012	Custom apparel	Custom		$1,600	$2774
6/13/2012	Fabric	Inventory	$685		$2089

Receipts

Even if you do not have time to organize your receipts immediately, keep them all. Not only will you need these receipts if you are ever audited, but if you have a return or factory warranty on a defective product you will need your receipt. I use two boxes, each the size of a shoebox. I put all of my receipts into box number 1. When I have time to sit down and log them into the computer, the receipts go from box 1 to box 2. This is a pretty simple procedure and also keeps clutter from building up.

If you are looking to mainstream your receipts and cut down on the clutter, consider scanning all your receipts into a filing system on your computer, similar to your paper files. There are systems you can buy that come with a small scanner and a filing system in place, but you can very easily set up your own. Any scanner will do. Start a new file under your documents named Receipts and then add separate files within the Receipts file. These are the files I would add:

- Office supplies
- Sewing supplies
- Fabric
- Equipment
- Travel
- Fashion shows
- Photo shoots
- Marketing
- Extras

You will end up adding more files, but this will get you started. Simply scan each receipt and add to the appropriate folder in the file. Date and name the file so you can easily find it later if needed.

Cloud Storage

You might have heard the term *cloud* being thrown around without reference to the white puffy things in the sky. They are referring to cloud storage, which is a form of saving files and backing up your computer to an invisible hard drive. You never see this hard drive, it's just there. This off-site storage system is maintained by a third party, and there is usually a monthly fee associated with the amount of storage needed.

At first I was a little leery. What if the files are stolen? What if the system crashes or the company disappears? Then the day came when I turned on my computer, and the screen was black. Sure enough my hard drive had crashed. Fortunately, I backed up my computer to a portable hard drive every week, but I still lost all the work I had from the previous five days. I was complaining to Deepika Prakash, CEO and founder of PatternReview.com, and she mentioned using a cloud storage. She has been doing this for a while, and every night their computers are backed up. So I decided to do a little more research and realized not only can I back up my information every day, I can upload files that I am not currently using, thus opening up space on my hard drive, and I can access this information from any computer. So here is a short list of pros and cons:

Pros

- It opens up space on your hard drive, allowing your computer to run faster.
- You can access the remote database from any computer.
- It allows others to access the data, which is great if you have employees or need to share a large file with a vendor or client.

Cons

- Who owns the data, you or the server?
- If you cannot afford to keep up your payment, do you lose everything?
- What if the server is hacked?

Despite the negatives, cloud storage is being used by many companies. So the question is not *if* they are going to use it, but *how*. Even with my skepticism, I am utilizing cloud storage, but I also have a portable hard drive that I back up and save all my files to first.

Optional Cloud Storage Servers:

- JungleDisk.com
- Rackspace.com/cloud
- JustCloud.com
- Cisco.com/go/cloud
- Carbonite.com

Accepting Credit Cards

If you are selling a product, you really have no choice but to accept credit cards. It makes it easier for your clients, and often it's to your advantage because some people spend more when using a credit card. Another positive is that funds are immediately deposited into your bank account, which saves you the time from going to the bank and waiting for a check to clear.

PayPal

By now you have probably purchased something online and were required to pay through PayPal. PayPal has made a reputation for being a secure way to pay for items online, and if you decide to sell on eBay you will have to accept payments through PayPal. It is very easy and free to set up your account, although it is not free to accept credit cards. Just like all the other companies, PayPal charges a percentage per transaction. Be sure you set up a business account and not a personal account; this will help keep your professional image when accepting payments on your website, eBay, Etsy, or wherever you link your PayPal account.

Intuit

Intuit offers a credit card service for your business that allows you to accept payments in person, on the phone, or online. I used Intuit for quite a few years. For a minimal fee I purchased a credit card swipe that hooked into the USB port on my computer, and because Intuit is linked to QuickBooks, it made it very easy to keep track of which clients had paid. The downfall was the high monthly **fees**, hopefully through time Intuit will reduce those. With my business operating in cycles, for the months I had very few transactions (or none), I was charged a monthly fee along with another fee for not maintaining a minimum charge quota. Eventually I stopped using Intuit as my main credit card company, but I do use them to accept credit card payments over my BlackBerry. This service does not charge a monthly fee.

UPS

We think of UPS as a shipping service, but surprisingly they offer packages with many services, including accepting credit cards. If you do not ship your merchandise, this will not fit into your business model, but if you are shipping, especially overseas, you will want to look into what they have to offer. Accepting credit cards and a special insurance on accepting COD payments are a few of the perks. You can contact them at UPS.com or monitor the Fashion Business Incorporated (FBI) website (www.fashion bizinc.org) for free seminars on this topic. On a side note, if you are a member of FBI, UPS offers a shipping discount as well.

Local Bank

The bank where you set up your business checking account probably offers options for accepting credit cards. If they don't, I guarantee you there is a bank in your local area that does. Depending on how much business you do with the bank, you might get a special deal or discounted rate. Again, be aware of any hidden fees, such as a minimum charging quota. You do have the option of negotiating the fees and rates, but do so before you sign any contracts.

Sam's Club

This one might surprise you, but Sam's Club offers quite a few perks with their business membership: Offering a merchant account is one of them. They offer very competitive rates and their customer service is top-notch. When you go to their website (www.samsclub.com), there is a section under Services where they have detailed information regarding their merchant program, along with a contact number, which is definitely worth the call. At the time I spoke with them, they offered different plans depending on the size of your business and the amount of charges you expect to bring in during any given month.

Portable Wireless Options

Many credit card companies can cater a plan for a small business, but before you sign up for a particular service there a few other things to consider. Will you be selling your line at trunk shows or trade shows? If so, you will need a wireless credit card machine. Before you spend a lot of money on a wireless credit card device, take a look at Square and Intuit GoPayment (see above). Both companies offer an attachment to your smartphone for accepting credit cards on the go. The credit card swipe attachment and the app are free, and the processing fees are minimal. This is an easy way to get started accepting credit cards at any location.

Inventory

According to the IRS, an inventory is necessary to clearly show income when the production, purchase, or sale of merchandise is an income-producing factor. If you must account for any inventory in your business, you must use an accrual method of accounting for your purchases and sales. To figure taxable income, you must value your inventory at the beginning and end of each tax year. These are the items you would generally include in your inventory:

- Merchandise includes the following: purchased merchandise; finished items that you have not yet shipped or that have not been paid for; any items that you have out on consignment; finished product that you have for sale in a display room, merchandise mart, or other booth.

    Do not include the following: items that have been sold and shipped, products consigned to you, supplies ordered for future delivery, supplies that do not physically become part of your finished product, and assets such as equipment (sewing machine, serger, mannequins, etc.).

- Raw materials
- Work in process, including indirect cost, direct materials, direct labor
- Finished products
- Supplies that physically become a part of the item intended for sale

Valuing Items in Your Inventory

You can see from this list, as your business grows, keeping close tabs on your inventory is very important and can get rather complicated from fabric that has just arrived, to samples you are in the process of making, to finished garments that have not been shipped yet. So how do you determine the value of each stage of your garment? There are two general ways to value your inventory: the cost method, and the lower of cost or market method. Here is a quick rundown of both:

Cost Method

Include all direct and indirect costs associated with each item:

- The inventory price of the items on hand at the beginning of the tax year
- Merchandise purchased throughout the year including shipping or other fees associated with purchasing the product
- Merchandise produced during the year including all direct and indirect costs associated with that product
- Any discount offered to you when you purchased supplies (for example, quantity discount or pay with cash discount) must either be included in your inventory tally or you must include them in your gross income

Lower of Cost or Market Method

For this method, you will compare the market value of each item on hand on the inventory date with its cost and use the lower value as its inventory value. You can use this method for items purchased that you still have in stock, items

Expert Tip

Make sure your inventory practices remain consistent from year to year.

that are currently being manufactured, and items that are finished but still in your studio.

Hiring

Eventually you will get to the point where you cannot do everything yourself, or you might even be working on a project where you need someone with expertise, such as a marketing expert or web designer. You can either hire a subcontractor or an employee. There are specific rules that apply in order to help you classify your worker. The government has three categories to determine if a worker is an employee or subcontractor:

- Behavioral control
- Financial control
- Relationship of the parties

Subcontractor

In regards to the three categories listed above, if you give a worker a deadline and allow them to work at their own time utilizing their own skills, this would qualify as a subcontractor. When hiring a subcontractor, you will pay them an hourly rate. You will not withhold any taxes from their pay, as it is the subcontractor's responsibility to pay their own income tax and self-employment tax at the end of the year. It is your responsibility to send them an IRS Form 1099-MISC, claiming what you have paid them for the past year, if you have paid them $600 or more. It is a good idea to fill these forms out the first week of January and get them into mail to each subcontractor, because they are due by February 28 to the IRS.

Employees

If you control the instructions of what the worker is doing as to how, when, and where, along with supplying them with on-site training, this would classify your worker as an employee. Another factor would be if you offer employee benefits such as health insurance, pension, or paid vacation time. There is definitely a lot more paperwork involved when you have an employee. You will need to withhold income tax, Social Security tax, and Medicare taxes from your employees' paychecks and in return pay this to the government. At the end of the year you will give each of your employees a W-2 form. There are services that you can hire to take care of payroll for you, including your bank and accountant.

Tax Deductions

One of the many reasons it is important to keep good records and receipts is to keep track of what you can claim as a tax deduction. For an itemized list of deductions refer to IRS.gov/tax or check with your accountant, but here is a rundown of some of the main deductions.

The House

When you are self-employed and you work out of your home, you can deduct a percentage of your house. If you have enough other deductions, however, I would avoid this one, especially if you file your own taxes. I have been told that there are many technicalities when writing off your home, as far as how much space and whether you use that space for anything personal. Writing off too much of your home can wave red flags at the IRS and give cause for a full audit. I'm not saying you are not telling the truth, but if you have enough other write-offs, why push the envelope? On the other hand, I would definitely write off the extra business insurance you have added. As long as you have a good accountant, they will advise you correctly.

Mileage

I usually carry a small notebook in my car and record mileage for any business trips I take. This does not just include traveling to an airport on my way to a conference, but even trips to the fabric store to pick up zippers or thread. You will be amazed how quickly your mileage adds up.

Equipment

Keep an ongoing record of any new machines or equipment that you purchase or sell. Allow your accountant to keep track of this for you, as some of your equipment needs to be depreciated over time. Any maintenance or repairs to your equipment can also be noted as a deduction. This includes sewing and office equipment: sewing machines, pressing equipment, computers, printer, and so on.

Telephone/Fax/Internet

If you have installed a separate business line in your home, you can deduct this on your taxes as a legitimate business expense. You may not deduct your home phone. You can also deduct Internet expenses and cell phone usage, as long as you use them both for business.

Memberships

All of the membership fees that you pay to any of the business, fashion, or sewing organizations are considered deductions. With that being said, if you go to any of their conferences or workshops, this is also a deduction, including the cost of the conference, travel, hotel, and meals.

Books and Magazines

In order to keep up in the fashion world, you will most likely have subscriptions to many fashion magazines and publications such as *Women's Wear Daily*. All of these subscriptions, as long as you are using them for business, should be noted as a business expense and an annual write-off. This is the same for any books you purchase; again just make sure it is something related to your business.

Fashion Shows

Fashion shows are a part of marketing, and you can write off these expenses. If you do a fashion show as a fund-raiser for a not-for-profit business, you can deduct all the expenses, including some of the cost for the garments if they are strictly for the event. So if you make a few "wow" garments that you want strictly for the fund-raiser runway show and have no intention of selling, that is a full write-off.

Business Expenses

Costs associated with running a successful business, from marketing to PR to bookkeeping—anything that costs you money to run your business—is a deduction, including these examples:

- Marketing your products with a mailing: the cost of printing the postcards and stamps
- Fashion shoot: the cost of models, photographer, makeup and hair, and so on
- Computer software and software upgrades
- Business cards
- Website hosting and domain fees
- Printer Ink
- Buying a new computer
- Charitable contributions
- Income (wages)

- Taxes and interest
- Child care
- Continuing education (Whether you take college classes or online seminars, most of these are write-offs as long as they help in your business. The small business seminars might only cost twenty dollars each, but these are also write-offs.)

Finding a Qualified Accountant

When you are self-employed, it is really a good idea to have a qualified accountant take care of your taxes for you. I'm not saying that you could *not* do it by yourself, but as a self-employed businessperson you are already on the radar screen for the IRS. By having an accountant go over your taxes, you are showing that yours is a professional business and you are taking extra care to make sure that your taxes are figured accurately. As a small business it will cost you a few hundred dollars a year, but in the long run it can save you time and money. Make a few phone calls and interview local accountants. Describe your business and see if they are knowledgeable about your specific record-keeping needs, such as inventory and samples. As a new client, some accountants will even offer to help you set up QuickBooks or a similar bookkeeping system for you. In the long run, the more organized your record keeping is, the easier it is for them to do your taxes at the end of the year.

When working from your home, you might be tempted to bypass some legal aspects of running a business, in particular care and content labels. You might think that you are starting so small, who will ever notice? You will be surprised how quickly things can develop in your business and when things start rolling you are not going to have the time to reorganize these legal matters. For example, in California and New York it is illegal to manufacture apparel from your home. This is a very important legal matter that needs to be addressed before you get your business going. From zoning issues when working from home all the way down to the labels that you need to put in your garment, pay close attention to the information in this chapter.

Zoning Issues When Working from Home

Before you set up your business from home, it is important to check with the local government regarding zoning laws in your area. This is even more important if you have clients or employees coming and going from your home. All you need is one phone call from a neighbor annoyed at the traffic going in and out of your house; if you have not gone through the proper channels, this could end up being a problem.

Contact the local zoning board or the planning department and ask for a copy of your jurisdiction's ordinance. If it turns out that the laws are not favorable for you to run a business out of your home, you can always consider appealing to the zoning board. If you do this you will need to explain if you will be seeing clients in your home, if employees will be working out of your home, and what hours you will usually have traffic. These are some of the main triggers that could cause a neighbor to contact the zoning board. You might also consider obtaining signatures from your neighbors stating they do not mind that you will be running a business from your home.

One last factor to keep in mind is how much of your house you are using for business compared to actual living space. This is referred to *space percentage*. As I mentioned earlier, my first two years in business my entire house was covered with fabric and work. At the same time, I did not have clients coming into my home: I picked up and delivered everything. I never deducted use of my home on my taxes, I did not have employees, and the few neighbors that actually knew I worked from home had no problem with what I was doing.

Trademarks

According to the United Stated Patent and Trademark Office (USPTO), an agency of the Department of Commerce, a trademark is a brand. A trademark or service mark includes any word, name, symbol, device, or any combination, used or intended to be used to identify and distinguish the goods/services of one seller or provider from those of others, and to indicate the source of the goods/services. Although federal registration of a mark is not mandatory, it has several advantages, including notice to the public of the registrant's claim of ownership of the mark, legal presumption of ownership nationwide, and exclusive right to use the mark on or in connection with the goods/services listed in the registration.

There are many trademark symbols that you are probably familiar with: McDonald's, Coke, Disney, Nike, and Polo from Ralph Lauren, just to mention a few.

There are two main symbols that relate to fashion designers representing a trademark:

- ™ represents an unregistered trademark or trademark is in the process of being registered; this mark defends your new symbol.
- ® is the symbol used for a registered trademark.

Do You Need One?

I did not trademark by name or logo for the first years in business. I focused my business on custom, one-of-a-kind garments with my mostly local clientele. At that time I did not sell on the Internet nor receive any publicity that would draw attention to my label. It was not until I decided to branch out into ready-to-wear that I filed for my trademark, and I was very grateful that nobody else was using my name.

If you plan on selling your clothing line on a national or international level I would definitely recommend applying for a trademark immediately. You will need to do a search to make sure that no one else has registered the name you have chosen or has a registered logo similar to yours. If you are going to sell your apparel in different countries, you will need to register your trademark in each country. You can apply for a European Economic Community (EEC) registration that will cover you in all of the EEC countries, which currently include Belgium, Denmark, France, Germany, Greece, Ireland, Italy, Luxembourg, the Netherlands, Portugal, Spain, and the United Kingdom.

Getting a Trademark

A trademark will cost you around $500 and you can apply for it by yourself online at USPTO.gov, or ask an attorney to file for you. By using an attorney, you can be sure that all the paperwork will be completed accurately, and they can also search to make sure you are not infringing on someone else's trademark. After filing for a trademark, you should receive a response from the USPTO within approximately three months of filing your trademark application. There is a free search application on the government website if you want to check if your name (or the trademark you desire) is even available.

Copyright

The definition of a copyright is a person's exclusive right to reproduce, publish, or sell his or her original work of authorship including literary, musical, and artistic work.

Do not let the term *artistic work* confuse you. You cannot copyright your garments. This becomes very obvious when we can see gorgeous couture gowns walking down the red carpet and wake up the next morning to find knockoffs available for sale. It can be very discouraging to know that you can put hours into a design, someone else can copy your design and sell it, and you have no recourse. Take a look at Forever 21: As of October 2011 the retail giant has defended itself against more than forty copyright infringement lawsuits. Most of the cases have been settled out of court, but the ironic part is that they continue selling apparel that is an exact replica of other designers' work.

Stay abreast of new laws regarding copyright in the fashion design world, as there have been some strong pushes, with the most recent one initiated by the Council of Fashion Designers of America (CFDA), for the government to allow fashion designers to copyright their work. On July 13, 2011, a bill titled Innovative Design Protection and Piracy Prevention Act was introduced to the US House of Representatives.

As a small designer, we almost have to look at this in a different light. It would be very frustrating to have your designs ripped off, yet the legal fees associated with suing a large company for stealing your work would be astronomical. So think of it this way, if somebody is copying your work that means that you are designing something that sells; take it as a compliment.

Back to the "authorship of artistic work," there are a couple of fashion-related items that you can copyright:

- Fashion design sketches
- A print design on fabric
- Unique website design
- Photographs

Getting a Copyright

It is fairly easy to apply for copyright, and you can do so online at the electronic copyright office (www.copyright.gov/eco). As of January 1, 2012, the online filing fees are a minimal thirty-five dollars, and response time for online filing is around three months. The website walks you through the process very clearly, including uploading any pictures or artwork that is needed.

Patent

A patent is something you apply for in order to have the right to exclude others from making, using, or selling an invention or product that you have designed or invented. Patents can end up costing quite a bit of money, not to mention that if you are fortunate enough to be approved, there are maintenance fees every few years. The patent process takes a long time to solidify, so be patient.

Traditionally, fashion design garments cannot be patented. Yet Joi Mahon, fashion designer and owner of Dress Form Design Studio, LLC, invented a unique functional feature to an outerwear garment that she decided to patent. I interviewed Joi in order to give you an insight as to what the process really entails. Joi explained what is involved, what the entire process ended up costing her, and how long it took her to finally receive a patent.

The Patent Process

As stated above, the goal behind patenting an idea or even applying for a patent is to protect your idea. Other options are to license your product and even sell the patent to a larger firm. This was one of the reasons Joi and her partner decided to apply for a patent. Although her item is clothing related, it has a *functional usage*, which are the key words here and why she was eventually awarded her patent. When Joi first decided to patent her item, she contacted one of the many inventor services that we see advertised on TV. This ended up being a costly and time-consuming business decision, and Joi encourages anyone desiring to apply for a patent to hire a legitimate patent attorney as your first step. When looking for a patent attorney, make sure the attorney is registered with the US Patent and Trademark Office.

Stats show that only a very small percentage of patents applied for are granted from the government. Joi finds this very important for you understand before you apply, so you are not discouraged in case your patent is turned down the first time. You do have one opportunity for rebuttal, which is another reason Joi recommends hiring a qualified patent attorney. How your patent is written is paramount in the success in getting your patent.

After moving on to a new reputable attorney, it took Joi three and half years and close to $10,000 to receive her patent. Initially, Joi produced her product, and now she is currently in the licensing phase of development.

Copying Other Designers' Work

If you venture into the custom-apparel side of fashion, you will inevitably have clients that will bring you photographs of high-end couture garments that they expect you to copy at a lesser price. The first few times this happened to me, I explained to the client that I do not copy other designers' work, but I would be more than happy to design something with a similar style. A common response was, "I have seen your work. I know you can copy this design." And I would reply, "There is no doubt I could copy that design, but I will not copy other designers' work. If you want that exact design why don't you just purchase it from the designer?" And nine out of ten times the response to that question was that the couture garment is too expensive; they were hoping I would make it cheaper. Ah, there is always a catch, so my final reply would be, "What makes you think I'm less expensive?"

When you are first getting started in business you might be tempted to take a job like this. If your goal is to become a fashion designer, regardless if it is in a ready-to-wear line or custom couture, copying other designers' work is not going to make a name for yourself. This is not to say that you cannot copy the quality of construction techniques of other designers. I learned all of my couture sewing techniques by studying other designers' work, either through books or examining the garments myself. As my earlier response stated, just because I know the couture sewing techniques that go into a particular garment, does not mean I will copy their exact designs. Eventually, I initiated a flat-out policy that I will not copy other designers' work. I posted a little sign on my wall and included a disclaimer on my website. This left no room for wasteful discussion.

So what if somebody brings you a photograph from a magazine with the design they want you to make? Politely explain that you do not copy other designers' work and begin to sketch a design with a similar style, but not exactly like the photograph. Many times, the client would end up liking my design even better than the one in the photograph. Keep in mind, you can see the client face-to-face. You see her body shape, and you probably can quickly form an idea of what style would flatter her best. Use that to your advantage.

Ethics versus the Law

Although the current laws do not protect a fashion designer with respect to their clothing, with such a strong push for new laws I find it hard to believe that there will not eventually be something put into place in regard to blatant copying. But as a fashion designer, there are certain principles that you should put into place regardless whether the law tells you to or not. We all use other designers' work as inspiration, but copying another's work detail for detail is simply unethical.

Clothing Labels

The Federal Trade Commission (FTC) has very strict laws regarding which labels you need to have sewn into your garments:

- Care label
- Fabric content
- Country of origin
- Identification of manufacturer, importer, or other dealer

Here are two publications (and their websites) where you can find specifics regarding the product you are making:

- *Threading Your Way Through the Labeling Requirements Under the Textile and Wool Acts* (http://business.ftc.gov/documents/bus21-threading-your-way-through-labeling-requirements-under-textile-and-wool-acts

Here are examples of the labels that I typically use in a garment.

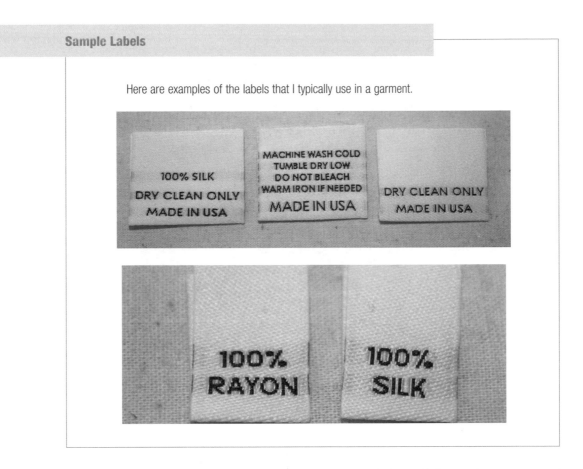

- *Clothes Captioning: Complying with the Care Labeling Rule* (http://business
.ftc.gov/documents/bus50-clothes-captioning-complying-care-labeling-
rule#Complying% =20with%20the%20Rule)

Care

When you order your fabric, you will be given the fabric content and care recom-
mendations from the supplier. This does not mean that you cannot change the care
instructions. For example, I use a lot of silk charmeuse that has a recommendation to
dry clean only. I then take the silk charmeuse, hand-dye the fabric, and then machine
wash and dry the fabric. I then choose to label my garment with this care label: HAND
WASH IN COLD WATER AND TUMBLE DRY ON LOW HEAT. The care labels are so your client knows
what to do with their garment.

Your care labels must be permanently sewn into the garment in an area that is easy for the consumer to locate. If for some reason you need to attach the care label in an area of the garment that is difficult to find, you need to add additional care information on the hangtag or on the packaging of the garment. If your garment is totally reversible without pockets or your garment can be cleaned in any way, including machine wash, tumble dry, dry cleaned, bleached, and ironed, you can get away with using a temporary label. If your client brings you the fabric and you custom make a garment for them, you are not required to insert the care label.

The FTC has a list of care symbols used by the American Society for Testing and Materials (ASTM) that can be used in your labels, but if you use symbols you must also have a written description either on the hangtag or somewhere else on the garment. A copy of these symbols can be found at www.ftc.gov/opa/1996/12/label.pdf. According to the Federal Trade Commission there are five elements that need to be addressed in your care label:

- **Washing by hand or by machine**—You must also give a water temperature setting if regular use of hot water will damage your garment.
- **Bleaching**—If your garment can be washed with any commercial-grade bleach, then you do not need to include anything about bleach on the label. Otherwise you will need to label it with ONLY NON-CHLORINE BLEACH, WHEN NEEDED, NO BLEACH, or DO NOT BLEACH.
- **Drying**—This is where you indicate how the garment should be dried and at what temperature. TUMBLE DRY LOW HEAT, HANG TO DRY, and LAY FLAT TO DRY are some of the common drying techniques you will see listed.
- **Ironing**—If regular use of an iron will not harm the product you can leave this off the label. The same applies if your item is wrinkle-free and you will not need to iron.
- **Warnings**—If there is any care that could harm the garment, you need to list that on the label. The same goes if care of one garment can harm another garment, for example, WASH WITH LIKE COLORS or WASH SEPARATELY, just the same as DRY CLEAN ONLY lets the consumer know that washing could damage the garment.

Fiber Content

You must include the fiber content, including the fiber name and percentage, for example: 90 percent cotton or 10 percent spandex. You do not need to include the content for select trimmings including braided trim, collars, decorative appliqué, and belts, to name just a few. You can also find an entire list on the FTC website. If your garment is decorated with an appliqué and the appliqué does not cover more than 15 percent of the garment, you do not need to include the fiber content of that particular appliqué, but you could include EXCLUSIVE OF DECORATION or EXCLUSIVE OF ORNAMENTATION on the label.

Country of Origin

This is particularly important if you have your clothing manufactured overseas. This label will need to be intact and is required by customs. If you are to use the label MADE IN THE USA, the entire garment, fabric and construction, must be American. If you are having your garments manufactured in the USA, yet you purchased fabric from overseas, than your label would read MADE IN THE USA OF IMPORTED FABRICS.

Identification of Manufacturer, Importer, or Other Dealer

For identification you can either use a company name or registered identification number, or RN. If you plan on using your company name, the name must be the same name that appears on your business documents as it cannot be a trademark, brand, or designer name, unless that is the same name you are doing business as. You could also use an RN, which is free to apply for at FTC.gov. The RN takes up less space on your label, and it is an easy way to identify you in the industry. For example, my label name is Angela Wolf, and my doing-business-as name is ABO Apparel, LLC. I can either include the ABO Apparel, LLC name inside my garment or my RN 137258, the RN takes up a little less space yet still does the job. If you go to the FTC website you can search under my business name or RN and you will know where the garment was manufactured.

There are other restrictions for this labeling. I encourage you to visit the Federal Trade Commission's website and visit the Frequently Asked Questions section, scrolling to the bottom for a link to the guide *Threading Your Way through the Labeling Requirements under the Textile and Wool Acts*. They have a PDF file that you can print for future reference.

Additional Label Information

There are three additional labels to include:

- Size
- Designer label
- Hangtags

There are many places that you can purchase these labels, just keep an eye on the prices. I have had good luck with PrintPlace.com. As far as the care labels, there are basic paper labels that can be sewn into the garment or the nicer woven labels.

Sample Additional Labels

Here are examples of a size tag, designer label, and hangtag that I use.

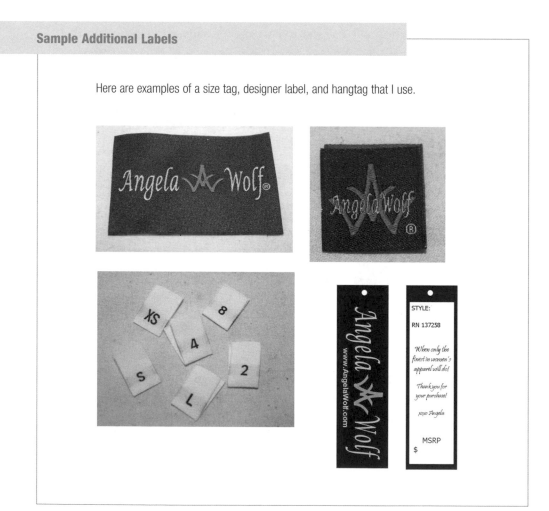

Regardless of what you choose for the size, fabric, and care labels, take extra care in choosing your designer label. This is the label with your name or the name of your collection that is always placed in a prominent position on the garment. This label needs to represent your brand. If you have a logo or a certain font used when representing your name, be sure to transfer that to your labels. Many of the label companies will allow you to upload a JPEG that they can copy onto your labels.

Once you start scanning a price list associated with labels, you will see a drastic difference between the cost of a printed label and a woven label. Choose whichever quality is cohesive with your brand image. If you are selling $3,000 jackets, by all means you better have a beautiful woven label.

The Law and Fines

You might think that as a small designer, no one will notice if you do not include the appropriate labels. That is not true. The current fine is $16,000 per offense, and the government does not care how big (or small) of a company you have. In fact I recall a story of a small designer in New York that was selling her clothing line at a few small boutiques. She was caught selling her clothing without content and care labels, and the fine was so steep she ended up going out of business. For the minimal cost of the labels, do not let this happen to you.

09

Social Media Marketing

Most people see social media as a way to keep in touch with family and friends. Although the names of the social media sites may change through time, the concept is here to stay. In the past, advertising has always been a one-way message; by one-way, I am referring to a magazine ad or a TV commercial. This type of advertising allows you to portray your product or brand to the public in any way you like, but does not allow consumers to respond to your message. On the other hand, social media offers a two-way message stream by allowing customers to personally interact. Social media has made such an impact on the way we do business that larger companies now hire social media experts. These experts spend their entire day online interacting with clients personally, forming customer relationships, answering questions about their products, creating buzz about new products, responding to complaints, and more.

From a business standpoint, social media offers a priceless opportunity for you to interact with your clients, draw in new clients, and get your name and brand out into the public—all without costing you a cent. With a simple click of a mouse, your message or product can be seen around the world. As a new designer and a small business, you must take advantage of social media marketing.

This does not mean you need to have a face on every social website. Every week I receive an e-mail from a new social interaction website; if I were to create a presence on every one of these I would spend my entire day on the computer. Keep in mind, every site will require some of your time: There are questions to answer, comments to respond to, and basic interaction with your fans and clients. I have listed and discussed my current favorite sites, but like I mentioned earlier, the website names may change (remember Myspace?), but the social media concept will only compound on what is already available.

Facebook

With over eight hundred million active users, Facebook is a perfect place to start. Facebook is a great place to post pictures or videos of your work, promote an event (such as a fashion show), and get your name out as a fashion designer. Remember, social media marketing is a two-way conversation. If others ask questions or make comments on material you post, make sure you answer them. You might even try to engage them in a conversation, and there is a reason behind this. Not only does this make you more accessible but the more comments you receive, the higher your message will show up on the home page.

I went to a seminar about social media marketing and the first thing the speaker said was, "Do you ever wonder why every time you turn on Facebook, you see postings from the same people despite the fact you have hundreds of friends and fans?" Then he explained the mathematics of engaging your followers/readers. When you post a comment or photo to Facebook or any other social media outlet, it is simply a post. With every comment you receive, your post rates higher and higher. The higher your post, the more people will see it. This expert discouraged people from only posting business material. When you first get started in your business, your posts are new and exciting, and your friends will be thrilled to see what you are doing, and they will comment like crazy. If you never waver from business, eventually you will lose your following, and your ratings will decrease. He gave ideas for other posts to engage your followers. For example, people love animal stories, especially when cats are involved. This guy would go out of his way to get a photo or video of his cat doing crazy things and then post it to Facebook or YouTube. By doing this, he would engage his audience on a personal level and receive numerous comments, thus popping his postings right to the top of the home page of his friends and fans.

Facebook offers several ways for you to establish a presence. Here are a few in more detail:

Personal Profile

A personal profile is required before you can access any of the other opportunities on Facebook. This profile requires others to "request to be your friend" and for you to "accept their friendship" before you are allowed to interact with each other. This profile is more about your personal life and gives you the opportunity to connect with friends and family. This does not mean you cannot post business messages on your personal page, but try to keep your personal profile just that—personal.

Create a Page

Creating a page allows any Facebook user to "like" your page. You will often see the "like" button on a website, a blog, or an advertisement. You can create a page for a business, an organization, a brand, a person, a particular cause, even a community event. You can have as many pages as you would like. Set up one page with your name as a designer and another page with your company, whatever best suits your business. For example, I have listed my Angela Wolf page as a brand. I do not have a page with my business name, ABO Apparel, LLC, because I thought it would be too confusing for my clients and fans, and I did not want to split the number of fans among two different pages.

Group

Many of my fashion designer friends started a group to go along with their fan page. A group offers a few perks that a fan page does not. For example, if you have an upcoming event, you can send an e-mail to everyone in your group. A fan page does not offer mass e-mail. Another feature is that your group can be public or private. Maybe you want to create a private group and invite your best clients. Call them your VIPs and use the group board to relate messages about new items you have made, private sales, or a preview of your new collection.

To get started you will need to create a personal profile if you do not already have one. Go to Facebook.com, fill in the required fields, and click Sign Up. You will be taken through a question-and-answer process to help create the profile that is best for you. Do not worry if you do not have answers to all the questions; you can always go back later and adjust your profile. You will also need to decide if you are going to keep your profile public or private. I personally keep my profile private, allowing only friends and friends of friends to view my pictures and comments. My fan page is public, and that is where I prefer my clients to interact with me. Once you have your personal profile set up, log out, reopen the browser Facebook.com, and underneath the sign up button, click on Create a Page.

There are opportunities on Facebook to purchase advertising for your business. You can also pay to create a "badge" that will show up on random Facebook users' pages. Facebook will focus your advertising dollars on select user profiles and locations depending on your product and business. Although I have not used this feature to advertise, this is something to keep in mind for the future. You can quickly and easily create an ad, and the best part is that you will only be charged if someone clicks on your ad. When discussing advertising on Facebook the question often arises, "How often do you click on the side ads?" Never—but that is not the point. It it does not cost you anything until someone does click, your ad is still right there all the time.

Facebook Posting Guidelines

The layout of Facebook continues to change, but the basic viewing options remain consistent. As you scan the news-feed area, take a look at the posts that are showing up on your wall. Which ones do you tend to notice first? I am guessing you are going to say the ones with video and pictures. Keep that in mind with your posts. Also consider the time of day you post your comments. If you are trying to hit a local market, post your listings in the morning, the noon hour, and after dinner. Unless you have something fabulous going on at the time, it is a good idea to limit your business posts to one or two per day. If you choose to post many listings on one day, spread the posts throughout the day. If you post all of your comments at the same time, your listings will be condensed, and you will not receive as good coverage as if you had spread them out over time.

Twitter

Twitter is considered microblogging. It's different than Facebook in that anyone can follow you and you can follow anyone without approval. You are limited to the amount of words you can use, so the theme for Twitter is more of a quick statement with a link attached to the rest of the story. Twitter recently added capabilities to upload photos or video to your tweets, which makes it a little more fun. The platform of Twitter is more like reading the classifieds in the newspaper—brief and to the point without a lot of visuals.

Setting up your own profile will take you only a few minutes. There are ways to customize the colors and background for your site, so consider uploading a photo of your dress form or something fashion related. Even if you do not have much to tweet about, Twitter is a great place to follow others in your field or other areas of interest.

Twitter Posting Guidelines

If you enjoy making comments all day, Twitter is the place to do it. There really are not too many guidelines to follow when posting your tweets, but in general three posts a day will maintain your presence. The good news is that Twitter has a seamless interface with your smartphone, so you can tweet from anywhere or schedule your tweets ahead of time. Twitter has an additional business resource website, business.twitter.com, that has free information on how to use Twitter to grow your business. There is also a free download for the *Twitter for Small Business* guide. The PDF walks you through setting up, explains the lingo of Twitter (hashtags, mentions, retweet, etc.), and offers suggestions on what to tweet and how to engage your audience. This is well worth the read!

Blogging

A blog is the perfect place to write or teach, comment on a specialty of yours, or showcase your expertise. There is no limit on writing space, and blogs can include pictures and video. For example, if you keep up on the hottest trends each season, your blog should be filled with pictures from the runways shortly after fashion week. If you just learned a new sewing technique or want to teach others what you know, your blog is the perfect place for this. People love free lessons, and the more you share, the more followers you will gain.

There are numerous websites that help you set up your own blog for free, including Blogger by Google and my personal favorite, WordPress. WordPress has all the built-in tools to create a highly visible blog, and you can adapt the pages into a website as well. When you sign up for a blog, you will be walked through the process of setting up your profile with a picture and bio. I have found the tutorials on WordPress to be an invaluable tool while changing the look of my blog. Similar to a website, you can choose your own design and layout for your blog. You can add your own logo as a header, change all of the menu options from a standard template, and adapt the background color, just to mention a few. One of the most important things to do is to link your blog to your website, Facebook page, Twitter, YouTube, and any other social media where you might have a presence. By linking your social media together, every time you post a new blog, the new message will appear on your other linked sites. Keeping this in mind, you might not want to link *all* of your social media because you may have different strategic marketing plans. For example, I link a live Facebook and Twitter feed that consistently runs on the front of my blog, but I do not allow my blog posts to automatically post on my Facebook page. After I post a blog, my update will show up immediately on Twitter, and then I go to HootSuite.com and schedule the blog post to appear on Facebook a week or so later. I do this because many of my Facebook fans are also subscribers to my blog. Instead of inundating them with the same message on the same day, I choose to spread it out a little. Just test the waters; you'll find what works best for you.

Blog Posting Guidelines

A blog differs from Facebook and Twitter in that your fans can enter their e-mail address in order to be notified of every new blog you post. I personally do not want to receive more than one new blog post per day from anyone. If you saturate everyone's e-mail with too many new postings, not only will they get sick of you but you could possibly lose followers, which contradicts why you are writing a blog. I try to post a quality sewing lesson or fashion tip once a week. On the other end of the spectrum, it is important to post frequently because search engines will pick up on your new content and continue to give you added Internet exposure. This is vital in increasing your online presence. Another way to increase your exposure is to add the option to "share link" at the end of each post. This allows your readers to share your new post across their own social sites.

Sample Blog Post

Website

Setting up a website has already been discussed in an earlier chapter, but it is important to understand that your website is the main hub for all your other social media efforts. Make sure you have a direct link from your website to all of your social media outlets; many of your clients will only remember your website name, and this will allow them to stay connected with your new activities. One more important feature to have on the front page of your website is a place for your followers to sign up for your newsletter and e-mails. This is where you will start to collect a client database. If your business entails sewing and fashion, many of your fashion followers will not be interested in learning to sew. I make it a point to find out if each new follower would like to be part of my e-mails regarding sewing, or e-mails regarding my new collection, or both.

Google Analytics

Your website will also be a good place to analyze how much traffic you are creating to your website from all of your social media efforts. Google Analytics, a free application at Google.com, offers you insights into the demographics of who is visiting your website, how long they are spending on your website, all the way down to which pages they click on. Google Analytics works by placing a tracking code on the front of your web page, and then Google collects and processes all the information. Start by setting up a Google account with all of your business information. You might already have a Gmail account or YouTube site; these will all be linked when you are finished. There are many products offered through Google, but this one is under Analytics, found by clicking Business Solutions on the bottom of the home page. Sign up your new website (or websites), and you will be given a code to attach to your site. Most website software will have Google Analytics applications built in that you can easily access. As soon as your code is attached to your website, you will begin seeing results within a day. There is a dashboard that displays how many visits, and those visits are broken into unique visitors and repeat visitors, even what country they are from. Use this information in order to continue to make your website better and better, and you will come to know your audience.

While you're signing up for Google Analytics account, you will also find access to Google AdWords, which basically advertises your business online. I am sure you have seen these ads anytime you have searched Google for a topic. Usually the top three or four businesses listed are paying for that placement. The little boxes to the right are also similar advertisements. Similar to advertising on Facebook, your ad will only show up when people are searching for a product similar to yours, and you only pay when your ad is clicked on. So how do they know if your product matches someone's search? Keywords. You choose the keywords that represent your business; these might be product names, your business name, or a larger category that envelops what you do. If you are having a hard time figuring the keywords appropriate for your business, Google will help by offering suggestions. How much will this cost you? You decide how much money you want to spend. This could be daily, weekly, monthly, whatever; you name a price and once your ads have received their budgeted clicks, your ads will not show up again until you decide to repay. When you get started you might want to give yourself a daily budget, which will give you new promotional opportunities every day.

Keywords

When designing your web page, you will be asked to name each page. Choose these names carefully, because these will be keywords representing your website. For example, if you name the first page of your website Home, those keywords are not going to help you out in the Internet search at all. Instead you might want to name your first page the same as your business name. The same goes for all the other pages: What words you use for the title of the page can help get your website to the top of search engines. You can also add tags or keywords to your website. You will simply list all the words that represent you and your business. If you are creating the website yourself, you will find most software will probably have these categories filled in with their business information, so just change it to your own.

YouTube

If you have the capabilities, you might consider putting together a short video to post on YouTube. A video of what you ask? Fashion show videos are great marketing tools. Once you upload the video to YouTube you can share the same video in your blog, Facebook, Twitter, and on your website. Teach a new sewing technique or post a video on fitting a muslin, or anything in the line of your business that could draw attention to your talents.

If you decide to post numerous videos, YouTube allows you to create your own channel. Think of this as a mini website. Take a few minutes to set up your own profile where you can upload your logo and include a description of your business. Any video that you create and post will show up on your channel.

YouTube is not just for posting videos; it is a great place to follow other fashion designers and learn from their work. On YouTube, you can search any topic or designer name, and you will see a list of videos to follow. Looking for inspiration? Take some time and scan some of your favorite fashion designers' latest runway shows. The potential lessons are endless.

Passwords

Speaking of passwords, it is not a good idea to use the same password among all of your social media sites. If the unfortunate situation came about that your site was hacked, the intruder would have access to all of your sites. This also goes with your e-mail accounts. All of my passwords are different, and I keep them in a small address book.

Creating a video is quite simple with today's technology. You can even snap a video from your smartphone, and with a few clicks your video can be uploaded to YouTube, Vimeo, your blog, Facebook—you name it. There are a couple of things to keep in mind when creating a video: Make sure there is good lighting and speak clearly. If you really want to have some fun, edit your video with special moviemaking software. This software allows you to add transitions, titles, music, and more. Again, choose your video title wisely and add tag words that will draw an audience to your product. Keep your videos short, under three minutes; you lose the attention of your audience quickly with every minute past that. It's not surprising with our busy lifestyles that our attention spans are very small, so make sure all of your relevant information is presented right at the beginning.

LinkedIn

Considered a professional networking site, LinkedIn has over one hundred million members. Just like the other social networking sites, you create your own profile. This profile consists of your current and most recent jobs, personal talents and expertise, and any achievement or awards that you have received. The best way to get started on LinkedIn is to gather all the information about your business, and possibly other jobs you are currently holding or have had that you want people to know about. Go to LinkedIn.com and fill in your name, e-mail address, and choose a password. The website walks you through setting up your personal profile. This website is a professional business site, so take some extra care into what photo you upload as well as the other information you share. LinkedIn asks for a lot of information in order to set up your profile, so don't feel like you have to finish all of it right away. A picture, description of your business, link to your website and other social media sites are just fine to start out. You can turn your profile to private if you only want your connections to see what you have to offer. This is really up to you.

Think of LinkedIn as a way to make connections in the fashion world from other designers, store owners, manufacturers, and fabric reps, to mention a few. If you end up looking for a job in the fashion industry, the connections that you make through LinkedIn are a great place to start your job search.

Groups

One of my favorite features on LinkedIn is the groups. You can search all groups by name or topic. For example, Independent Fashion Designers is the name of a group that I recently joined. Then there are the groups that you will recognize by their name, such as Fashion Group International or Association of Sewing and Design Professionals. The groups can be a resource of information along with a perfect way to meet others in your field around the world. Show your expertise when the opportunity arises.

Pinterest

You have probably seen the little logo that reads PIN IT. This is an innovative, fun, and easy way to share pictures from the Internet with your friends and fans. Pinterest is like an online bulletin board. Each member can create their own bulletin board topics—as many as you want as a matter of fact. As you browse the Internet you can "pin" images or videos to your boards. To sign up, you must have an invitation or go to Pinterest.com and request an invitation. Trust me, with all the other social media you are going to be working on you will get plenty of invitations. My invitation came through Facebook, so when I created a profile in Pinterest, I was able to link to all of my Facebook contacts. The same goes along with Twitter. Making a profile is very simple: Create a username and password and you are on your way to beginning your boards. Do not worry if you cannot think of any board titles yet; you can change them and add new ones at any time.

Now, Pinterest does not just have to be filled with pictures of your own clothes, although I hope you will have a board filled with your sketches and designs, but think of other fashion designers that inspire you. Go to shopping websites and pin some of your favorite styles for the season, new colors, and upcoming trends. This website allows people to re-pin what you post, and the better job you do, the more followers you will acquire. Think of this website as 100 percent eye candy.

Create a Social Media Marketing Campaign

In relation to how much content you should share at any given time, compare the social media websites to a meal: Facebook would be a heavy appetizer, a blog would be the main course, and Twitter would be your after-dinner drink. Keep this format in mind as you create each new message. Creating a social media marketing campaign can be focused around a new event (your fall fashion show), a new product you are launching (a new T-shirt line), or simply a way to create some buzz around your business. Regardless of the reason for your campaign, creating a viral buzz makes it look like things are happening in your business, and people want to be part of new and exciting things.

Creating the Buzz

I was preparing to show my couture collection at a local art museum, and for the opening reception there would be a live photo shoot. One of the gowns I was designing involved over eighty hours of hand beading. My goal was to create a social buzz around this gown, which would show what goes into my couture gowns and draw people to visit my exhibit. I started the buzz by posting one picture of the front of the sheer bodice wrapped in a beading hoop; all you could see was basting thread showing where the design would go along with a handful of beads. The next picture was taken three days later, with the gown on a mannequin. I had made pretty good progress beading, but if this gown was going to be on a person for a live photo shoot I had a long way to go, and the photo on the mannequin showed this. I posted the picture in the early evening and by the next morning my Facebook stats showed over 1,200 clicks just on that picture alone. By the end of the week stats showed over 10,000 clicks. The dress became known as "the gown," and I still receive comments about all the hours of beading.

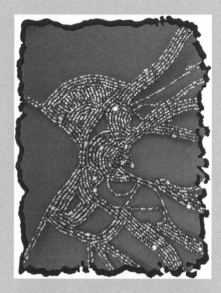

Do not post generic phrases. Engage your followers and show your true personality behind the face of your business. You might consider posting pictures of the new fabric you just got in or talk about the inspiration for your next collection. If you are working on a large project, update with pictures as a status report; your followers will love that.

Viral Marketing

Viral marketing is what encourages your fan base to pass along your message. The quality and creativeness of your message will determine your pass-along rate (or how quickly your message spreads from person to person or how quickly it dies). In short, viral marketing is a way to get your message or product out to the public by word of mouth utilizing your social media outlets. This is such a great opportunity for new fashion designers to get their image and brand into the hands of potential consumers. Just like the example I gave (see page 155) with the beaded gown, create your own viral marketing campaign around your own product or service. For example, if wedding gowns are going to be your focus, video record and photograph one of your gowns from start to finish. Plan a schedule to post updates about your gown. You will be surprised at the amount of people who follow your progress, maybe even a few who want to purchase your final design.

Scheduling

If I have a fashion show coming up or something exciting going on in my business, I will sit down with the calendar and lay out a schedule for my posts. It is important to plan the schedule in advance, because once you get into the thick of finishing your project or finalizing your collection, social media marketing will be the last thing on your mind when in fact it should be first and foremost for marketing.

I print a six-month calendar and use colored markers with abbreviations to remind myself which days I want to post where:

- An orange *B* for blog
- A light blue *T* for Twitter
- A dark blue *F* for Facebook
- A black *L* for LinkedIn
- A pink *W* for my website

Scheduling like this keeps your social media sites up-to-date and current with what is going on in your business. For example, every Friday I have an orange *B* circled on the calendar. This reminds me to update my blog and check my stats. Even if I have nothing to say that week on my blog, it keeps me on my toes and thinking of something to teach or show my followers the following week.

I schedule at least three business Facebook posts a week, which might include updated pictures of my new clothes or online sewing classes that I am teaching at the time. Every week I make a note to login to LinkedIn and see what is going on in the groups I have joined.

Combine Them All

If you really have a lot going on and have difficulty finding the time to do the social media marketing, consider scheduling your messages using online software. Online software programs allow you to write out your posts and schedule the time your message will appear on a select social media site. This is an easy way to be able to schedule your posts in the morning and evening hours when many of your followers are online, even if you cannot be.

Here are the two that I use:

- **TweetDeck.com**—TweetDeck can be viewed online, or you can download the interface to your desktop. On one screen you can view all of your Twitter feeds and mentions, Facebook newsfeed and messages, and even schedule your posts to Twitter and Facebook. TweetDeck is very user friendly, and you can quickly schedule all of your posts for the day or week.
- **HootSuite.com**—HootSuite encompasses most of your social media on one website. This is a fast and efficient way to scan and post to Twitter, Facebook, LinkedIn, Foursquare, Ping, Myspace, and WordPress (to mention a few). You can schedule a message months in advance as well as keep an eye on stats for each of your sites, all from one location. HootSuite is very user friendly and offers a paid subscription as well as a free subscription. I have always used the free subscription.

Stay Focused

There are other websites that offer scheduling and stats for your social media sites, just Google "managing social media" and you will find many options, along with many new social media platforms. As I mentioned earlier, the websites for social media might change and expand; in fact as I am writing this chapter I have invitations to join friends on Google+ and Tumblr, but try to focus your attention on a few select sites. It is better to narrow your focus on one or two sites and maintain your presence on that particular site with quality content than to scatter yourself everywhere. Not only will a narrow focus help you to manage your message and brand image but you will attract followers much faster.

10

PR, Marketing, and Advertising

With your business set up and social media outlets ready to go, what kind of message are you going to put out there. First and foremost you need to create a brand, and everything after that will relate back to the brand image. All marketing and advertising efforts must portray your brand in a light that will help you to build a clientele and following. Be consistent!

Branding

Branding is so important and something you need to take into consideration from the very beginning. Ask yourself what the image is that you want to relay about your clothing. What are the qualities or values of your brand? For example, will your clothing focus on a casual, relaxed style as we often see in California or more of a formal European styling seen in New York?

In building your brand you need to figure out your brand's best characteristics and create a brand promise. Some examples would include high-end women's apparel with quality fabric and construction, or affordable, unique T-shirts always using ecofriendly fabrics. Once you have this established, you must consistently deliver what you promise. If you promise the best quality, every garment that goes out your door must be the best quality. If you promise ecofriendly fabric, you must never create a T-shirt with a polyester. Consistency! Once you have established your brand, consistency will be the key to your success in maintaining a certain image. Consistency in price, quality, and fit are vital. For example, if your focus is on premium denim, and your jeans sell for $300 a pair, you will really confuse your client base if all of a sudden you sell a style that runs $40 pair under the same label.

Logo

Create a logo to represent your brand and image. Take into consideration the name of your business and play around with different colors, labels, and tag-lines. Also, make sure you are not copying another logo. Looking for inspiration? Check out the logos of some of the most recognizable fashion labels: Chanel, Coach, Louis Vuitton, Ralph Lauren, Calvin Klein, just to name a few. There are many different software programs that can help in laying out a logo, including Adobe Illustrator and CorelDraw. But if you don't already have those programs, take a peek at LogoMaker.com; they offer free templates and layouts to get you started. In fact, take a quick walk through your local office supply store and you will find a variety of logo-creating software. Once you have a logo, you should apply for a trademark on it (see chapter 8). Use your logo on everything: your labels, business cards, business letterhead, invoices—everything.

Business Cards

One of the first marketing tools you need to have in hand, *always* in hand, is a business card. In fact, just last week I ran out of cards, and I felt naked. Of course, that evening I had two different requests for my business card, and I had to resort to scribbling my number on a napkin. The first thing I did when I got home was to reorder more cards. I hope that never happens again. When designing your business card, make sure to use your logo, but at the same time create a color scheme and style that represents your brand. Check out Vista print.com for great prices on printing. If you are still unsure about a logo, they have many creative templates to choose from. On your business card make sure to include important contact information: business name, your name, phone, address, e-mail, and website. If you do not want people to know your address for some reason, then have two cards made. When you go to a trade show you will need to give your address to the vendors you order from. It is so much easier to hand them a card with all the information than to fill in the left-out information.

PR

Everything you put out to the public should relate to your brand. From the logo to a signature look, your brand should tell a story. Public relations is strategically increasing awareness about your brand. Keep in mind that you are not just selling a product, you are selling a lifestyle. So the question is, are you going to hire someone to get your name out to the press or you going to do it yourself? PR firms can be quite costly, with basic fees starting around $1,200 a month. That can put quite a dent into your financial budget when you are first starting out. Other than taking a toll on your time, there is no reason you cannot start out by doing your own PR. It is free, and you control the message, not to mention you can build relationships with select magazine and newspaper editors, as well as other stylists, which can prove to be a great asset to your publicity.

First, make a list of any of the magazines, newspapers, TV, radio, and blogs that you would like to get your name into. Be selective, always keeping your brand in mind. Gather names of the editors or columnists that you need to contact. Put together a press kit, including a short bio about yourself and information about your designs and send it to each contact. If you do not hear back in a few weeks, send them another e-mail asking if they received your package. Give them something exciting to write about; the press loves featuring new designers.

And never miss an opportunity to promote yourself, especially if you have a fashion show coming up or just won a contest. As a new, small designer, the newspapers are not going to chase after you for an article. The year I won the Passion for Fashion contest in Novi, Michigan, I made a visit to a local newspaper's office. I told them that I am a local fashion designer who had just won a national design competition. They were thrilled to be able to write a story about somebody local. In fact, I received a full two-page spread, with photographs, featured in a Sunday edition. That is priceless, free advertising.

As a new designer, at first you have a better chance of getting your name out to your local community. Newspapers have a fairly short lead time, so you can approach them with a story or an event and make the pages of the paper in a week. With any press you do receive, make sure you post a link to your website and social media sites. Local recognition—even on a small basis—can expand to national recognition quite quickly.

Press Release

A press release is a document used to communicate news to the media announcing something exciting: the launch of a brand, a new collection, or an upcoming fashion event. When writing a press release, make sure there is an interesting story angle and a great pitch. Include a strong headline and make sure the who, what, where, when, and why are in the first paragraph. Be sure to include your logo and any relevant images. Send out a press release e-mail to the editors individually; if you do not hear back, pick up the phone and call them.

Here is a sample of one of my press releases for a fashion show:

Sample Press Release

PRESS RELEASE
FOR IMMEDIATE RELEASE

Contact: Nancy McDonnall
Public Relations
ABO Apparel, LLC
(555) 555-5555

MEDIA ALERT
WHO:
Angela Wolf

WHAT:
Wine, Women, and Music—SW Michigan Symphony League Charity Event
Full runway show featuring Angela Wolf Couture and the launch of the Angela Wolf Spring/Summer women's RTW line
Guests enjoy wine, hors d'oeuvres, and live music.

Kindly reply by the 24th of March to NancyMcDonnall@qtm.net—(555) 555-5555

WHEN: Thursday, March 25
6–8 p.m.

WHERE:

The Heritage Center
601 Main St.
Saint Joseph, MI 49085
Phone: (555) 555-5555

Award-Winning Designer Angela Wolf in Sold-Out Charity Fashion Show

ST. JOSEPH, MI — The Symphony League of Southwest Michigan will feature national award-winning fashion designer Angela Wolf of ABO Apparel in Wine, Women & Music, a spring fashion show, on Thursday, March 25, at the Heritage Center in St. Joseph, Michigan.

This first-time, women's night-out fund-raising event for the League sold out just days after it was announced locally on the group's website that the launch of Angela Wolf's women's Spring/Summer Ready-to-Wear collection will be featured. Over two hundred and fifty tickets were sold and over one hundred women are on the waiting list to attend. Many of the women who couldn't get tickets quickly volunteered to help serve wine and food and other tasks in order to attend.

Angela Wolf has specialized in custom couture for over fifteen years. An A-list clientele throughout the United States has helped to build this designer's reputation and is one of the many reasons the anticipation of her RTW line is so intriguing and well received.

Angela is a local fashion star who has won several national fashion-contest awards. At the fall American Sewing Expo, the largest independent consumer sewing expo in the US, Angela's line, Angela Wolf Couture, was featured. She has also won the top award in the Passion for Fashion challenge at the American Sewing Expo, and in her debut appearance she won Audience Choice Award for her design. Angela has also graced the cover for the Expo's brochure.

"I personally want to thank all of my clients for allowing me to do what I love most, being able to dress a woman in a way that enhances her individual beauty."

—Angela Wolf

For interview opportunities with Angela Wolf or to attend the show please contact the Director of Public Relations, Nancy McDonnall with NMAC Marketing Consultants: NancyMcDonnall@anysite.net or (555) 555-5555.

About ABO Apparel, LLC
ABO Apparel, LLC is a fashion design house and atelier for the Angela Wolf label.
The ABO Apparel design studio is located at 185 East Main St., Studio #102, Benton Harbor, MI 49085, (555) 555-5555.
Contact Angela Wolf at pr@angelawolf.com.

# # #

March 15, 2012

Putting Together a Press Kit

Make your life a lot easier and prepare a press kit to have on hand. I have read this in many books, and I found it to be absolutely true. The time will come that you will receive a call from a magazine or newspaper that wants a quick snapshot of your brand or your clothing. That does not sound so bad, but they usually want it immediately. Depending on your workload, it might be very challenging for you to drop everything in order to prepare this, but at the same time it is an opportunity you cannot afford to miss. So take the time now and put together some information.

A press kit should include the following:

- Photos
- Any press you have received
- Link to your website
- Links to all social media sites that you might maintain (Facebook, Twitter, YouTube, etc.)

Pitch Letters

A pitch letter is a brief letter, usually one page, that accompanies your press release or press kit. The whole goal is to pique the journalist's interest, almost like a teaser. You should include a catchy subject line, photos, and links, and then get straight to your message, letting them know that you will call to follow-up.

One Sheet

A one sheet is a burst of information about the brand or designer, specifically created for sales or advertising. When the media calls and wants additional information, this is what you send them. By taking the time in advance to prepare this, it will look more professional, and you will not miss the message you are trying to send. Within this one sheet you should include the following:

- Your business name and logo
- The name of the clothing collection
- Background on the designer
- Photographs
- Links that you find important to your message
- Other press you have received

www.AngelaWolf.com

When only the finest in women's apparel will do!

About: Fashion designer Angela Wolf started ABO APPAREL, LLC in 1994 with the main focus on women's higher end, custom couture and has built an international A-list clientele. Angela just launched her first ready-to-wear collection and it has been met with rave reviews. The Angela Wolf Collection was created for a women's everyday lifestyle and is made up of separates consisting of beautiful luxurious fabrics paired with impeccable fit. Angela has a passion for developing new fabrications and techniques, all while keeping ahead of the fashion trends, which makes this collection one to keep an eye on.

Press: Winner of Passion for Fashion in 2008 and in 2010 Angela was named one of the featured designers in the Chicago Showcase by the Apparel Industry Board. Expanding her expertise into the sewing industry, in 2011 Angela became the couture sewing expert on the PBS series *It's Sew Easy* and is quickly becoming a household name.

Contact: If you would like more information or a current look book on the Angela Wolf ready-to-wear collection contact us at sales@angelawolf.com or visit www.AngelaWolf.com

ABO APPAREL, LLC   185 E. Main St., Suite 102   Benton Harbor, Michigan 49022 Phone: 269.556.9746
www.Angela Wolf.com   Email: info@angelawolf.com

The goal of the one sheet is to be flashy and stand out among other designers. You might want to include a personal tagline or an interesting twist to your overall story. Be authentic and intriguing.

Pitching

You can always pitch the media yourself, just like my example above about going to the newspaper myself. There are certain things that you can incorporate into your pitch that might intrigue some editor's attention, such as announcing a new clothing line or exciting news about you as a designer. Editors receive a ton of requests every day, so make yours pop. Tailor your news to their publication by referring to one of their past articles. Make sure you include photos in the e-mail and not just links, because many times they will not click on your links. Of course, if there are any celebrities that have worn your clothing, make sure you include that information, too!

Getting Your Clothing on the Right People

There is no better advertising than someone wearing your clothes. Word of mouth, especially in your local area, can play a big part in the success of your clothing line. So, you have finished your first collection and you have created some social media buzz, now it is time to get your clothing in the hands of potential clients. There are many ways to do this, so be creative.

Get Your Clothing to the Celebrities

Our society is crazed about who is wearing what designer and which designer is dressing which celebrity. All you have to do is glance through an issue of *InStyle* magazine, snap shots of celebrities on the street with taglines of "who" they are wearing. Can you imagine the impact on your clothing brand and sales if Jennifer Aniston was photographed wearing your designer jeans?

Celebrity Gifting

Do your research. Not every celebrity will wear your product, so you need to take that into consideration. Begin with the image of your product in mind, and then scout out which celebrity or public figure has the same style sense. After you compile a list, pick out the celebrities that you would like to see wearing your clothing. Research to find out who their publicist is (even better, their stylist) and contact this person to find out if that particular celebrity is accepting gifts. If gifts are accepted, prepare your package with detail. Do not waste this opportunity!

In your package include the gift for the celebrity along with a personal note. Include some information on who you are, what type of clothing you design, where your clothing is available to be purchased, your website, and other contact information. Tell them that you are a new fashion designer. If you strictly design custom clothing, let them know that what you have sent them is a one-of-a-kind garment. It is a good idea to also include a gift for the publicist. The gift does not have to be the same as what you are sending the celebrity, but give them something nice along with a thank-you note for accepting your package. Make sure you follow up with the publicist a few weeks later to make sure that they received your package.

Friends and Family

Some of the easiest customers to approach your clothing are your friends and family. Offer them a free top or a free pair of jeans in exchange for their feedback regarding fit and comfort, along with a commitment from them that if they like the product, they will spread the word.

Two things could come out of this exchange. They could love your product, and they will brag about the great fit and how good it makes them look. Or if for some reason, they really do not like your product, your family and friends will tell you the truth. Either way, it is better to know up front if there is an issue with your designs. On the positive side, there is nothing more rewarding than to have friends come over and try on your clothes and tell you how fabulous they feel, especially when you have been staring at these clothes for weeks. In fact, it is only because of my friends modeling in one of my runway shows that convinced me to pursue designing jeans. I had a few samples available, but I was really unsure about the fit of the jean. One after another, each one of my friends tried on the same pair of jeans, and they all wanted to purchase my sample. This is invaluable feedback and priceless advertising about my product.

Donations

Donating a product or service to a charity event can be good exposure. Keep an eye out for potential opportunities. For example, when I was first starting my business, I participated in a fund-raiser for the local college. Tickets sold for $150 a person, and the event offered a very formal dinner, silent auction, and live auction. Since I focused on custom apparel at the time, I offered a custom jacket, valued up to $750, as a live auction item. I placed an outfit on a mannequin for display, received a large write-up in the brochure, and because I attended the function, I had the opportunity to meet many of the guests and field questions about my custom apparel business. If you donate a custom service of any kind, make sure you have a price listed with your offer in order to protect yourself. I offered a jacket with a value up to $750, but that does not mean that the winner of the auction item cannot purchase one of my more expensive jackets—they would just have to pay the difference. This is one way to protect yourself from having to deliver more than you expected.

Once your business gets rolling, more and more people become aware of what you have to offer. It will not take long for the first call to come your way with someone wanting a donation for a charity event or fund-raiser. Before you accept or decline their proposal, ask a few questions about the event:

1. How many people are attending?
2. What is the average age of attendees?
3. Is the event geared toward women or men or both?
4. If you donate something, what advertising or publicity will you receive?
5. What exactly do they want you to donate?

These are just ideas of a few of the questions you could ask, but it is better to know up front if this donation will benefit you at all. For example, another time I donated an item valued at a few hundred dollars for a silent auction. It turned out that items in the silent auction were not listed in their booklet nor did any of the donors of silent auction items received any credit or recognition at all. This is how I learned to ask more questions when organizations come to me asking for donations.

One more key item in choosing where to donate for exposure is to consider the clientele that will be attending the event. Make sure the venue and event coincides with your brand image and the product that is being offered.

Look Book

A look book is basically a booklet or catalog of your current collection. The book can be used for promotional material showcasing your clothing, a vital instrument in selling to boutiques and buyers, and sent to magazines and fashion publications trying to get your line noticed. As a new designer there is no need to spend a lot of money; with a little creativity you can come up with something unique. The look book consists of photographs of your items usually shown on a live model or a mannequin, and it should give an overall feeling or mood of what your collection represents. Just make sure you use quality photographs.

As a new designer, there are cost-efficient ways to create a look book. Places like Snapfish.com and Walgreens both offer creative ways to make a book out of your photographs. Be creative, unique, and try to stand out from your competition, always making sure to incorporate the image of your brand into designing the book.

Create the Reputation

As you build your business, you will begin to find your niche. This is really important if you are focusing your business on custom apparel or alterations. If you design custom clothing your niche might fall in bridal, tailoring, or exquisite casual wear. Once you realize where your specialties fall, you want to create a reputation for being the best in that particular area. You can create this reputation through creative marketing and advertising, but there is no better way than word of mouth from your clients. How your clients perceive your talent and skill can really affect the growth of your business, so be sure to build a rapport with your clients, whether it be in person or through mediums such as Facebook.

Becoming the Best in Your Field

With so many designers and seamstresses, how will you ever know if you are the best in your field? You won't, but you can creatively put a message out to the public showcasing your talent. Whether through giving sewing tips, fitting advice, or fashion forecasting, every time you share quality information, you are giving yourself credentials. The funny thing is that the more advice you share, the more customers will rely on your services and, ironically, the more confidence you will build in yourself.

Entering Fashion Design Competitions

One way to get your talent noticed is to enter a fashion design competition. There are numerous competitions throughout the country, and with the popularity of reality TV, we seem to have another one added to the venue each season. There are also sewing and design challenges sponsored by magazines, fashion design colleges, and fashion-based organizations like the Apparel Industry Board and Fashion Group International.

Project Runway

Of course, one of my all-time favorites is the reality TV show *Project Runway*. Watching a handful of designers create a runway-worthy garment within a few hours is exciting and inspiring. The more the show becomes popular, the greater the reward for the designers to participate on the show.

If you'd like to try out for *Project Runway*, e-mail the casting company for an application form. The casting company can change, just the same as the hosting channel changed from Bravo to Lifetime, but you can start with Bunim/Murray Productions (www.bunim-murray.com) who cast the ninth-season contestants. The application is long and very detailed with questions regarding your personal life, family life, and fashion design aspirations. If you are invited to the casting call, you will need a portfolio and samples of your work. I actually filled out the entire application, and while debating if I should send it in a not, I met one of the contestants from season five. I asked him his least favorite part of being on *Project Runway*, and he said, "The lack of sleep, only four or five hours of sleep a night." Well that did it for me; no wonder the contestants break down in crying tantrums! So, for the second year in a row my application ended up in the trash. Maybe next year.

Fashion Star

Besides *Project Runway*, there are other reality TV shows featuring fashion designers. In the spring of 2011, there was a casting call for a new NBC series called *Fashion Star*. This show was cast by Kassting Inc. (kasstinginc.com), and their application process was almost identical to *Project Runway*'s. This series, which began airing in March 2012, focused on having a clothing line manufactured on a mass scale.

Passion for Fashion

Based on the concept of *Project Runway* with twelve final contestants, a challenge, and two days to create a look for the runway, Passion for Fashion is held at the American Sewing Expo in Novi, Michigan (www.americansewingexpo.com). This contest is similar to one episode of *Project Runway*. In order to apply, send in one of your finished garments along with an application. The deadline for entering is usually midsummer, as the expo is held toward the end of September. The winner receives a top-of-the-line sewing machine and a seven-day trip to New York with a private tour through the garment district. I won this contest in 2008, and the exposure I have received in the sewing industry since that time is priceless, not to mention the contacts I made in the garment district for fabric and trim sourcing.

11 | Selling Your Line

Any emerging new designer who decides to exhibit at a national trade show needs to be confident that they can deliver their product. They also need to reach out to potential retailers through direct mail or e-blasts to make appointments. Finally, they need to commit to more than just one show so that buyers see they have "staying power" in the marketplace. The trade show experience is a building process, and with the right tools it can be the key to success.
—*Susan Glick, Vice President, Women's Apparel Merchandise Mart Properties*

Getting your product on the sales rack is how you are going to begin generating revenue. There are so many options available to you, be creative and don't bite off more than you can chew. If you know you do not have the funds available to sell to the large retailers, it is better to hold off until you do. You can put yourself out of business faster than you can blink if you commit to more than you can deliver.

E-Commerce

Every year, the number of people shopping online and the amount of money spent through e-commerce increases. If you have a product to sell, it only makes sense to offer your product for sale online. With today's technology it is a reality that you can work out of a small room in your house and sell your product worldwide.

eBay

Whether eBay is a viable option or not really depends on the price point of your product. During the time I was personal shopping for select clients, I would end up with some leftover merchandise. Instead of returning the clothes, I would sell some of the designer brands on eBay. I found the overall process quite easy, but very time consuming. It seems the overall perception of eBay is that you are going to get something for nothing. A new designer does not have the reputation that will bring in the big dollars on an eBay auction, like Louis Vuitton or Chanel does. Fixed-price listings are offered on eBay, which is a little more economical, and you can ask a better price for your items without paying so much just to list your item. At the same time, eBay then takes a higher percentage of your sale.

So how does eBay work? During the years that I sold on eBay, they changed their policies quite a few times, and each change seemed to put the seller more at the mercy of the buyer. As a buyer, that is a great confidence to have, but in the e-commerce world, you as a seller are opening yourself up to many different obstacles.

Auction Listing

You have the option of listing your item as an auction or as a fixed price. Auction items are usually based on one-, three-, five-, seven-, or ten-day auctions, with seven days being the most common. Yet there is a strategy behind the number of days you choose for your auction. Your ranking on the eBay's search engine is higher the moment your auction starts and the final hours before your auction ends. For example, if you know that from Thanksgiving to Christmas is a high traffic season on eBay, you might consider utilizing three-day auctions in order to get more exposure for your items. Instead of an auction only receiving two days of higher rankings within a week during a seven-day auction, a three-day auction will give you four days of better exposure during a seven-day period.

There is also a strategy to the time of day that you list your item. If your highest ranking is going to be when your auction lists and when it ends, posting something at 2 a.m. drastically reduces your audience. For apparel, the ideal listing time according to TeraPeak.com is from 4 p.m. EST to 10 p.m. EST. I also noticed that my auction listings ending on Thursday and Monday evenings consistently brought in higher bids than the other days of the week. If you are using eBay to upload your listing, you can pay a fee to schedule your listing to start at a specific time. There are also other sites that offer online hosting to eBay, such as Auctiva.com, which I have found to be more cost-efficient and easier to use. For a minimal monthly fee, Auctiva offers great templates to choose from, picture hosting, and the ability to schedule your listings in advance. I could sit down for one evening and design and schedule my listings for the entire week—very efficient. Another benefit of using sites such as Auctiva to set up your eBay listings is that you can include as many pictures in your listing as you would like without paying the additional fee that you would through eBay.

Fee Schedule

When selling on eBay, keep an eye on the fee schedule as it changes every so often. You will be notified in advance of any price changes or listing specials. The insertion fee for listing an auction item on eBay (as of June 2012) is as follows:

$0.01–$0.99	$0.10
$1.00–$9.99	$0.25
$10.00–$24.99	$0.50
$25.00–$49.99	$0.75
$50.00–$199.99	$1.00
$200 or more	$2.00

This is the fee that you will pay to list your item on an eBay auction regardless if it sells or not. If your item sells, you will also be charged a final value fee, which at this time is around 7.5 percent. If your item does not sell, you may relist your item one more time with no insertion fee.

It is a good idea to print out the current pricing structure and keep it handy when listing items on eBay, because in the long run you can save quite a bit of money. For example, if you are going to list a jacket for $200, you would be better off starting your price at $199 because you just saved yourself a dollar for every time you list that jacket. One dollar might not sound like much at the time, but if you list numerous items throughout the year on eBay, you can save hundreds of dollars.

Buy It Now Pricing

Every item you place up for auction can also have a Buy It Now price available. Of course you will pay an additional fee for adding a Buy It Now price, but this is a way to cater to the shoppers who just want to purchase your item and do not want the thrill of an auction. This will also allow your listings to show up in eBay's Fashion Outlet, a new shopping experience similar to Amazon.

eBay Stores

If you find yourself listing quite a few items on eBay, take a look at the eBay stores available. This is an easy way to organize your listings in a professional format along with perks like reduced insertion fees and free use of Selling Manager, which enables you to automate much of your selling process. With an eBay store, you can list items as a fixed-price listing that enables your item to stay available in your store for thirty days with one listing fee. A basic eBay store has a monthly fee of $15.95 a month. With this subscription you will also pay a 20-cent fee for every item you list, along with a final value fee of 11 percent of the purchase price. I used an eBay store for years, and I found this to be a very easy and efficient way to be part of e-commerce. The downside is that as my business grew, many of my clients did not want to purchase my clothing through eBay.

What Does eBay Really Cost You?

After figuring the final numbers between paying eBay fees and PayPal fees, I found that I was paying back 50 percent of my gross sales. This figure remained consistent (between 50 percent and 51 percent) for three years in a row. Keep the 50 percent figure in the back of your mind as you are pricing your items. Once you have solidified a sale price for your garment, make sure you at least double that cost as a listing price on eBay or you will lose money all the way around.

There are positives and negatives to selling on eBay, and hopefully with each new change eBay institutes they will keep in mind the sellers that have made their website so successful. Their current rating program will probably hit a nerve once you start selling, especially when it comes to shipping, but at the same time, eBay offers a very easy platform for you to sell your items.

Etsy

Etsy is considered the world's handmade marketplace. Everything on Etsy is handmade by an artist or designer. There are three types of items that can be sold on their site:

- Handmade by you
- Crafting supplies
- Vintage goods (do not necessarily have to be handmade, but they must be at least twenty years old)

Etsy offers an easy and free way to set up your own store. You can add pictures and information about yourself and your business, create a circle of friends, and connect with other artisans. The current fees for Etsy are as follows:

- Twenty-cent listing fee for each item, and listing lasts four months
- 3.5 percent final sales fee

The fee layout for Etsy is quite a bit cheaper than eBay, and the consumers that shop at Etsy expect quality and uniqueness. All in all, Etsy is a great avenue for selling your garments.

Shopping Sites

As the e-commerce world continues to grow, more and more online shopping sites are popping up. Many of these are geared toward the smaller, up-and-coming designer. These sites offer inexpensive ways to sell your product through their online boutique. My new favorite is Shoppista.com. This site has a boutiquey feel. They market their website to the consumer, while offering a professional-looking base for your merchandise. While there are many of these sites popping up, make sure you check the Internet for positive and negative comments from consumers and sellers.

Your Own Website

Your website will always be your main marketing tool. Setting up your website as a full e-commerce site, apart from other selling sites, can be time-consuming and expensive if you are not careful, especially if you have to hire someone else to design and maintain your site. If you plan on designing an e-commerce website yourself, there are other websites that can assist and make this process easier.

Shopify.com and BigCommerce.com

Shopify and BigCommerce are just two of the many online services for creating an e-commerce website. They have different options, depending on how many items you plan on listing. The fees associated with this site are very reasonable, and you can sign up with your own domain name. Shopify.com offers very professional-looking templates to choose from, allowing your e-commerce to look just as professional as the big retailers.

Linking Other Selling Sites

The easiest way to sell your clothing on your website is to have a link from your website to your online shop at one of the other websites mentioned above. For example, on my apparel website, AngelaWolf.com, I list the pages that someone can click on across the top. One of the tabs says "Shopping." When someone clicks on this tab, a new window opens and they are taken to my e-commerce site on Shopify.com. Most people will not even realize they are on a different site altogether. I made sure to coordinate the color scheme and the design on my website and my other shopping sites. Also, make sure you include a Home button on all the pages so the consumer can always get back to your original website. Another example is my pattern website, AngelaWolfPatterns.com. I have linked this site to my storefront on BigCommerce.com. On your website, you can have as many links as needed. Maybe you have a page titled "What's New"; link that page to the new items you post on your Etsy store. Then set up a page titled "Sale Items" or "Sample Sale" and link that page to your eBay store, or in my case, Shoppista.com.

Utilizing the easy interface of e-commerce already available on so many websites will just make your job easier and more seamless when trying to maintain an online presence. One last thing: If you are currently selling your line to retailers, do not undercut their prices on your own website. This is highly frowned upon, and if the retailer discovers that you are doing this, they probably will not order from you again. For example, if a boutique that carries your line is selling one of your jackets for $500, don't sell the same jacket on your website for a penny less than $500. In fact, you should price it even higher at $550 or $575. Retailers that carry your line have enough competition, so they do not want to have to compete directly with designers themselves.

Trunk Shows

Trunk shows are one of the easiest ways to get your name and clothing into the hands of potential clients. Not only are you getting your product out there, you are adding a face and a personality to your label because you are there promoting and showcasing your own items. Trunk shows also give you a chance to see the reaction to your merchandise regarding style, price, and fit.

What Is a Trunk Show?

A trunk show is basically you introducing your merchandise to potential clients and buyers either at a store, a home, or another venue. Many designers use trunk shows as a way of showcasing their upcoming season collection to select clients, giving them the opportunity to purchase before anyone else. As a new designer trying to expand your clientele, I cannot think of a better way to get your product into the hands of potential buyers. Even better than that, the cost is minimal.

Private Shows

Have you ever gone to a Pampered Chef party or a Lia Sophia party? A trunk show is the same concept. Once you have enough items ready to sell, ask one of your friends to host a trunk show for you. Offer your friend a discount or free item in exchange for having the party at their house and inviting their friends. You might even offer to pitch in for wine and appetizers, just to make sure the trunk show is a fun party. Once you have scheduled the show, send out invitations and make sure you include an RSVP in order to have some idea of how many guests to expect. On the day of the trunk show, make sure you give yourself *at least* two hours to carry in your items and set up. In fact, when I have a trunk show in someone's home, I ask if I can set up early that morning. I usually have a lot of things to carry in, including mirrors, mannequins, and clothing racks. This allows me to get all the hard labor out of the way, and I have time to shower and get ready for the trunk show. Use the "Trunk Show Checklist" on page 179 to prepare for your show.

You can have the most beautiful clothing in the world, but it never looks as good on a hanger as it does on an actual person. Consider bringing along a couple of models or friends that fit into your clothing well. Throughout the trunk show, have these models walking around and continually changing clothes. This makes a huge impact, and I guarantee you will sell more clothing, especially if there are a lot of guests there throughout different rooms in the house.

You will also want to schedule a time to have all of the guests come into one room and give them a short presentation. Introduce yourself, thank them for coming, and take a few minutes to talk about your background and design philosophy. Let them know what you have to offer. Talk about your clothing: the fabrics you use, the fit of your garments, whether they are easy to care for and wrinkle-free or high-end and one-of-a-kind. As you are talking about your garments, take them off the rack and move them around, hold them up against yourself and give the garment some life. Pass the garment around so they can feel the fabric or look at your linings, whatever it is that you want them to remember about your product. Invite them to try on any of the items and let them know your order policy; is this a preseason sale where they

Trunk Show Checklist

Here is a checklist of items that need to be available at the trunk show:

- ❏ Mirror
- ❏ Clothing rack or racks
- ❏ Extra lighting (if needed)
- ❏ Receipt book and calculator
- ❏ Wireless credit card machine (options covered in chapter 7)
- ❏ Measuring tape (especially if you are taking orders for custom work)
- ❏ Pins
- ❏ Photo and sketches of your work
- ❏ Guestbook (for the guests to sign up for your e-mail and mailing list)
- ❏ Clothing for sale along with other fabric samples, if applicable
- ❏ Business cards

order now and you deliver six months later, or is this item available immediately? Make sure they know the timeline for delivering their product. And lastly, invite any of the guests to host their own trunk show.

As you expand your clientele you might need a larger venue for your trunk shows, especially if it is more of a VIP preseason show. Check out some of your local restaurants; many of them have separate rooms or areas in the restaurant that they will allow you to use. Although there might be a fee for the room, if you hold the show on a weekday afternoon and evening, the rate will be less—if not free. If you go this route, make sure your invitation says whether it is an open bar or cash bar.

Trunk Shows at a Boutique

Trunk shows inside of a boutique or department store are very common, especially preseason sales. By preseason sale I am referring to selling your clothing six months before it is delivered to the client. For example, you have your fall collection finished and ready for orders in March. You would schedule your trunk shows in April and

May, then take all of the orders and manufacture them throughout the summer so they are ready for delivery in August, or whatever date you have agreed upon with your client. The same process goes for your spring collection and holiday and resort wear, if you offer them.

As a new designer, you might have a challenge getting a boutique to purchase your clothing. Yet some boutiques will allow you to have a trunk show inside of their boutique; this way they do not have to purchase your clothing, and they will be able to see how their customers react to your collection. Do some research and find boutiques that carry clothing similar to what you design. Check the price points of their clothing, which designers they currently carry, and what type of customer base they draw. Only choose boutiques that are appropriate for your product. Once you have your boutique hit list, contact them and find out who their buyer is. Call them and offer to send them a look book so they can preview your product. If you cannot reach the buyer by phone or they do not return your phone calls, then go ahead and send them a look book and mark "Attention [the buyer's name]" on the mailing label.

When scheduling your trunk show, boutiques might want to schedule you for one day, a weekend, or an entire week. Make sure you find out what they are planning and make sure that the plan works for your schedule. Once you have your trunk show dates, include them on your website so your clients will know where to find you.

Price your product for a trunk show the same way you would price if you are selling to a boutique. Find out from the boutique what percentage they charge, typically 50 percent of the sale price, and that is what you are to add to your wholesale price. This would be the same retail math as if the boutique were purchasing your clothing line; they usually take your wholesale price and double it or even add a little more.

When holding a trunk show in a boutique, it is important that you are there and available to talk with the customer and market your clothing. Make sure you look nice and definitely wear one of your items. You are the image of your brand, so be approachable and personable and that will be your best advertising. If your trunk show proves to be profitable, the boutique will probably want to schedule you again and possibly carry your line in their store.

Online and Virtual Trunk Shows

Preseason sales are when you will make the best margin on your apparel. Your client will pay full price in order to be guaranteed a look from your new collection that they are being offered before anyone else. With the click of a mouse, you can offer clients worldwide a sneak peek into your new collection. Salvatore Ferragamo deserves the credit for launching the first online trunk show (for a sample of how their website is set up visit www.ferragamo.com).

You could easily set up a private trunk show just for clients with a password-protected e-commerce website. Only clients with this password would be able to enter and shop during that particular sale or fashion event. Shopify.com, among many others, offers a website with password-protection capabilities.

One website that allows you to create your own wholesale shop, free of charge, is Balluun.com. When you sign up you will add your business information along with photos of your items for sale. Similar to other social media sites, businesses will ask to connect and you can search out buyers yourself. It is like an online international trade show.

The Fashion Show

A fashion designer's highlight each season is to view their hard work gracing the runway with high-energy music and beautiful models. I must confess the runway show is my ultimate high, despite all of the work that goes into producing one. As a smaller designer, you might think having a fashion show is out of the question because of the cost, but that is not true. Although you might not be able to have all the decorations and stage lighting that you would like, you can still put on a top-notch fashion show. Planning a fashion show is really no different than planning a wedding reception: Finding a location, sending invitations, setting up a photographer and videographer, and decorating the venue are just a few of the major steps involved.

Planning the Show

There are really two types of fashion shows:

1. The high-fashion runway show with rows of seating
2. The casual show with seating at tables and models walking in between and around the tables

Both options are viable to showcasing your collection, and each option has its own advantages and disadvantages. Whichever you choose, use the fashion show to showcase your collection to the press, to store buyers, and to your clients.

The *runway fashion show* consists of rows of seating with the models walking either on a raised stage or on level ground through a path made by the chairs. When

True Story

I held a runway show utilizing the events room at a local college; this room caters to many wedding receptions and prestigious events. Holding the fashion show during the week tremendously lowered the price of the room rental, but what I was not prepared for were the additional costs that were attached to just about everything.

I knew this fashion show would cost me a little bit more because I offered an open wine bar and hors d'oeuvres. I chose this venue because of the large space, plus there was a runway they could set up, and I did not have to worry about hiring that out. They also offered great stage lighting that was built into the room and a fabulous sound system. What I didn't realize is that I would have to pay hundreds of dollars to utilize the sound system and stage lighting. The room rental fee was just that—a room. Everything else was additional. There was a charge to use the tables and chairs, not to mention that if I wanted a nice tablecloth, that was also extra. The room across the hall for the models hair, makeup, and changing area was going to add hundreds more, so I vied for black curtains behind the stage for only one hundred dollars. This was dark, ill lit, and the models were practically on top of each other. I am still amazed they came out wearing the correct outfits and accessories. And the runway . . . even though they owned the runway and offered the runway while I was scouting out venues, there is a charge for every four feet of platform. By this time, my budget was totally blown out of the water, so my vision of a forty- or fifty-foot runway quickly was condensed to eight feet.

On the day of the fashion show, I arrived to the venue and quickly realized that there were no decorations, thus no atmosphere whatsoever. It just happened that on the days I visited the room it had been set up for an upcoming event. In order to utilize their beautiful hanging lights and fabric swags from the ceiling, I was looking at another $500 to $700. You can imagine my dismay and annoyance by this time, but in the real world you need to make it work. And that is exactly what I did, but I learned a lot from this experience, and I will never allow myself to be put into that position again. I quickly realized why brides planning a reception are ready to pull their hair out by the time their wedding arrives.

planning the layout of your runway show it is important that every seat offers a good view of the models. Scan some of the fashion shows on Style.com and you will see the different layouts, backdrops, and runway platforms being used.

The *casual fashion show* is more interactive with your audience. The audience is usually seated at tables and the models mingle through the crowd, allowing your guests to get a closer look at the details and the fabrics you are using.

Whichever fashion show format you choose, just remember the main purpose is to showcase your collection and hopefully end up with sales.

Location

The first thing you will need to decide is which type of show you plan on having because this will have an impact on determining the location. A casual fashion show can be held at a restaurant or lounge; try to have the area to yourself. My first fashion show was held at a restaurant. I chose a weeknight for the show, and the restaurant did not charge me for the room because they assumed they would make up for it on alcohol sales, which they did. All of my guests were seated at tables, we had music (utilizing the restaurant sound system) playing in the background, and I provided the commentary for the show while models walked in between and around the tables. At that time I was focusing on custom, one-of-a-kind garments, and this was a very inexpensive way to showcase my garments and talent to potential clients. By choosing a restaurant location, there is no need to rent tables and chairs, which can save you a lot of money. Plus the restaurant probably already has a liquor license, which saves you another hassle.

A runway show requires open space and a decent-size room. This is a little more challenging to find, especially if you're in a small town. Venues that are used for wedding receptions are a good place to start, and if you have your fashion show during the week, the room rental will usually be considerably less. If there is a local college, see if they have a room dedicated for wedding parties. Many times they have a runway available along with the appropriate lighting and sound system built in, but usually with an extra cost.

While you are scouting out locations, have a list of questions that need to be answered at each location. This way when you make your final decision all of the costs are laid out accurately. Here is a list of questions to consider when looking for a potential location:

1. Is the location easily accessible to your guests?
2. What is the room rental fee? Are there any additional costs?
3. What type of runway will work in this venue?
4. Do they have any stipulations on what can go on the floor? For example, if you rent a raised runway, do you need carpet runners underneath to protect their floors?
5. Depending on your layout, how many guests will fit comfortably and do they have enough chairs to accommodate your needs?
6. Do they have a liquor license? If so, are you able to have an open bar or a cash bar? Will they allow a local wine distributor to donate wine to your event?
7. If you decide to serve appetizers or desserts, may you choose your own caterer or do you have to use their service? (Obviously, if you have chosen a restaurant as a venue you will be using their service. Do not offend them by asking this question.)
8. Is there a changing area for the models? Is there a charge for this extra room?
9. Can you set up your show the day before? (This is really important, especially if you are doing most of the setup. It takes a full day to set up, and you want to look fresh and clean at your show, not like you just finished running a half marathon.)
10. If you are planning an evening fashion show, will you need to tear down that night after the show or can this be done first thing the following morning?
11. Do they have a sound system that you can hook a microphone or iPod to? If so, is there a fee to use this?
12. Check out the lighting at the location. If the location is at a restaurant do they have dimmers on their lights or is the lighting so dim you will need to add spotlights? If the venue is at an auditorium or a place that specializes in shows, do they charge a fee to use their stage lighting?
13. Are there any additional costs that might pop up?
14. If the show is outside, is there a plan B if it rains?

After you have had a few fashion shows, you will add to this list of questions, especially if you have your fashion shows catered. Did you know that a caterer might

> ### Ideas on Locations for a Fashion Show
>
> - Restaurant
> - Bar or lounge
> - College
> - Country club
> - Popular wedding reception venues

charge you one dollar per plate? The list goes on. You still might end up with a few fee-related surprises at the end, but the fewer surprises the better.

Inviting Guests

Be sure to give careful attention when deciding whom to invite and how to invite them. There are several different options.

- **Invitation only**—When you are first getting started, you might consider an invitation-only fashion show where you invite your friends and clients and allow them to bring along a guest. This is a good way to have new potential clients attend your show, but at the same time give a feeling of exclusivity to your client base. This is also a way to control the number of attendees, in case the location of your fashion show is rather small.
- **Selling tickets**—If you are going to sell tickets to the show, make sure the price of the ticket coincides with what you have to offer. Are you creating more of an event, offering complimentary wine, hors d'oeuvres, and live music? Or are you simply having a runway show where everyone will be in and out the door in thirty minutes? You might consider choosing a not-for-profit or a particular cause to donate proceeds of the show to. In general, people are more inclined to rationalize paying to go to an event if they know they are helping or donating to a particular cause. Not only that, but if you team up with a not-for-profit and use your fashion show as their fund-raiser, the fashion show will not cost you a penny. Ticket money can be used to cover your expenses, and then the proceeds are given to the not-for-profit.

In addition, you can write off any other expenses incurred that were not covered, such as part of the cost of the sample garments.

- **The press**—Make sure you invite the press to your show. Take the time to scan local newspapers and magazines to determine who would be most likely to write something about your show. Send an invitation and follow up with a phone call to make sure they received the invitation. This also gives you a chance to personally invite them again. As a new designer, the press is probably not going to search you out. Therefore, go out of your way to offer them a complimentary ticket and front row seat. The more your name appears in the press, even if it is only in your local paper, the better.

Decor

Take a good look around the venue of your fashion show. What is the atmosphere like? Some places have their own ambience that you can tie your show into, while other places need decoration in order to create a mood. If your guests will be sitting at tables, what type of centerpiece does the venue offer, or will you need to create your own to tie into the theme of your show? Will you need tablecloths and flowers for the entrance table? Should you consider using mannequins dressed in your latest looks as an entrance? Decorating is something to take into consideration while you are choosing a location. If you are renting an empty hall, you could end up spending quite a bit of money on decor. On the other hand, if your fashion show is held at a country club, the mood and the decor might be sufficient for what you are looking for.

Runway

The location of your show and your budget really determine the type of runway you use. Do not be afraid to be creative and think outside the box. Unless you plan on building your own runway, you will need to rent the runway in order to have access to a raised runway. The cost of the runway will depend on how long it is, and this cost can add up quickly. There is also usually a delivery charge, along with a setup and breakdown fee.

- **Runway surface**—While you are checking the cost of renting a runway, find out if the runway is carpeted or raw, unfinished wood. When one runway I rented showed up, the surface so awful that I had to ask the photographer to take pictures from a lower angle so the floor would not be visible in the pictures. The photographs turned out terribly! Because the photographer was so low to the ground and angling his lens up at the models, every model looked out of proportion.

■ **Skirting**—Depending on the style of runway you are looking for, you will probably need to have some sort of skirting around the entire edge of the runway. This curtain usually clips or attaches with hook-and-loop tape to the side of the runway and can be rented by the foot. Again, if you are using a long runway, this cost can add up quickly.

■ **Floor runway**—There is nothing wrong with having a runway show without a raised platform; you just need to make sure you do not have more than two or three rows of seating or those in the back will not be able to see. In fact, if you look at some of the runway pictures from other designers, many of them have the models walking on the ground. On the plus side, by utilizing the floor you can design a much longer runway or different walking patterns that you would not be able to do with a raised runway. Take a good look at the floor and make sure this will show up well in your photographs. The floor can add to the effect of your overall theme, like an old-fashioned brick or painted cement floor would.

Models

You have a few options when choosing models, depending on your budget. If your budget is limited, consider asking friends that fit into your sample sizes. If you are really lucky, maybe you have friends with modeling experience. Another idea is to holding an "open call" for models, and in return they can use the photographs from your show in their portfolios. Models who are just starting out are more willing to work with you on a trade. Some of my fellow designers announce their model open calls on Facebook. You just need to make sure you have enough of a backbone to say no if one of the potential models will not work for your brand image. The same goes when asking friends to model for you; sometimes it is hard to say no because you do not want to hurt their feelings, but ultimately if the models do not show your clothing well, you will not end up with sales. In addition, the quality of the photos from your fashion show will be poor if the models do not show well, and the pictures will be useless for advertising purposes.

Hair and Makeup

When looking for someone to do hair and makeup for your show, start with some of the hairdressers in the salon you currently go to. Ask if anyone is looking to build their portfolio. Just like you offered the models, offer the photographs to the hair and makeup artists in exchange for their services. Word will travel fast about your upcoming fashion show, so if nobody in the salon you currently go to is interested, they might know someone who would be.

If it is the first time you are working with this hair and makeup artist, give them a photograph or magazine clipping of the makeup and hairstyles you are looking for. Ask them to do a test run on you or one of the models to make sure they can deliver the look you want. They might even have a portfolio of their work for you to view.

Photographer and/or Videographer

If you have to choose one area not to skimp on for the fashion show, it should definitely be in choosing your photographer and videographer. You might have friends just getting into photography who want to shoot your show, and there is nothing wrong with that. By all means invite them to photograph the show. But at the same time make sure you have a professional there as well. I am speaking from firsthand experience: There is nothing worse than going to all the work of putting on a runway show and ending up with terrible pictures. The whole purpose of your fashion show is to promote your brand and your clothing, and the best ways to do this are through pictures and video posted after the show. Bad pictures equate to no promo!

That being said, this does not mean that you need to spend thousands of dollars for quality photos and video. Just like I mentioned with the models and hair and makeup artists, there are photographers looking to expand their portfolio into high fashion. This works out as a perfect trade: You supply the models, the clothing, and the event, and they in turn shoot your show. Put together a contract that both of you sign, agreeing that you have full rights to all of the photographs and/or video. Photographers might even ask you to include their name below each picture you use for promo, which is a fair trade for their services.

Depending on the size of your fashion show, you might want multiple people taking photographs and video. I try to have a minimum of three photographers and two videographers. This will give you a variety of shots and behind-the-scenes footage to incorporate into your promo. This is also a safety net in case of the inevitable equipment failure or if someone does not show up.

Music

Your music needs depend on whether you are planning a runway show with the loud pumping music or resorting to soft, behind-the-scenes music while you are doing the commentary. Music can also be played as part of the atmosphere while your guests are arriving and mingling before the show starts.

- **Live music**—Contact your local symphony office and see if there are any high school members that might play the violin for an hour. Check with your local schools and ask about local bands; just make sure the type of music they play fits with your clientele. Have them play in the background while your guests are arriving or during intermission, if you have one. If you find somebody really good, you might consider having them perform during the fashion show.
- **DJ**—Hiring a DJ eliminates having to get a license to play certain music for your show. (If you play copyrighted music at your fashion show yourself, you would need to buy a one-day license.) A DJ will usually bring their own sound system, but you need to tell him or her in advance what and when you expect them to play. Have the DJ play softer music when your guests are arriving and after the show while your guests are mingling. Make sure the DJ knows what type of music to play since their taste might be totally different than yours. Weeks before the show provide the DJ with a song list or at least preview what you would like to have put together to play during the fashion show. The music has the ability to excite your crowd or put them to sleep; make sure you have the right concoction, and the DJ knows exactly what you are expecting.
- **Music mix**—Most of the sound systems nowadays offer the ability to hook into your iPod or MP3 player, which really makes it easy to put together a good fashion show with high-energy music. You can put together different playlists for different parts of your event. If you plan on using copyrighted music, you will need to get a daily license for each song in order to legally play it for the show.

Boutiques

As a start-up designer, boutiques are a very viable option to sell your clothing. But every boutique doesn't offer the same results, so it is your job to research the boutiques that will be a perfect fit for your clothing. Take into consideration the style of your collection and the price point, probably the two most important factors when searching for boutique. You do not want your collection to be the most expensive or the least expensive in any store. As your search for the perfect boutique narrows, think of how your items will look hanging in a particular store. Do you like the layout of the boutique; can you envision their clients wearing your clothing? What other brands do they currently carry? Are the brands comparable to what you have to offer?

Visit the store as a shopper and take note of the cleanliness, the dressing rooms, and the professionalism of the staff. Does the staff seem knowledgeable about the brands that they carry, and are they helpful in selecting merchandise for the clients? Is the staff friendly, or is the attitude more like they are doing you a favor by being open? It is challenging enough launching a clothing line, but if you do not place your merchandise into the correct store, not only will your clothing not sell but the boutique probably will not reorder.

Setting Up an Appointment

Call the boutique and ask the name of their buyer and explain that you are a fashion designer and would like to show them your new collection. If it is a smaller store, many times the buyer is also the owner. You can even share with them that you have visited their store and you think your collection will complement the other brands they carry. You might even add that you think your clothing would hang perfectly next to a certain designer. This shows that you are not just pitching every boutique, you have done your research, and you really believe your clothing will sell in their store.

What you can offer to a boutique to entice them to buy your collection is a faster turnaround than the larger brands offer. Maybe you can propose new deliveries each month, which will keep their inventory fresh without having to spend a lot of money months in advance. There are creative ways to get your foot into the door, but if your collection sells, that is only the beginning.

Selling Your Product

If a retailer has decided to purchase your collection, now it is time to educate the staff about your product. The more they know about your product (the quality of the fabric, hand-dyed fabrics, impeccable construction—whatever your signature is) the better the chance of portraying your brand in a way that will sell to the clients.

Make a habit of calling the boutique every week or two and checking to see how your product is selling. Do they need anything else or do they have any questions? Without being sand in their underwear, show them that you care about your product and you want to make sure it sells, which is a benefit to both of you.

Consignment

Consignment is when you supply product for a store and you do not get paid unless your item sells. The store will usually take an average of 50 percent of the sale price, so price your merchandise appropriately. I consider consignment to be the very last route in selling your product. I would dare to use the word *never,* but in today's business world, you should never say never. A store might offer to take your clothing on consignment terms as a way to see how your clothing sells in their store before they commit to purchasing your collection. This is a risk-free way for a boutique to test out a new designer. As good as that offer might sound, this puts you in a very difficult predicament. First of all, you need to supply merchandise to the store, and you will not get paid unless your product sells. This can tie up your cash flow for months, and depending on your budget, this can prove to be detrimental to your business. Another negative to selling your product on consignment is the dedication of the staff. If all the other products in the store have been purchased by the owner, the sales staff will be more enticed to sell those products over yours in order to get the money that they have already committed. It does not cost them a penny to have your items hanging. If your clothing does not sell, it's no skin off of their back. And lastly, if your product is not selling and at the end of the season you receive all of your merchandise back, what are you going to do with it? Not only are you out quite a bit of money, you are left with clothing that you can only hope to sell at a huge discount.

The only time I would even remotely consider a consignment arrangement would be if the boutique is exquisite and I am absolutely dying to get my product in there. This means I have researched and found an ideal match for my clothing, I will take the risk and supply them with product that I will only be paid for if it sells.

Selling to the Larger Retailers

As your business grows and you continue to gain a clientele, you might consider approaching some of the larger retailers, or maybe your vision is to sell to the larger retailer immediately. Either way, I would highly suggest reading *Fashion for Profit* by Francis Harder first and foremost. Her book offers insight into selling to the big guys and how to avoid the downfalls and financial catastrophe. Not to sound like a downer, but there is so much to take into consideration when selling to the larger retailers, and the more information you can gather the better. There are so many factors that are added with the larger retailer that you might not encounter with the small boutiques. For example, there are packaging, labeling, and shipping requirements. If your order

True Story

Many fashion-related business classes and seminars I have attended greatly discourage giving your merchandise to a store on consignment. Among other reasons I will share here, what if your garment is stolen or damaged? Who is responsible?

I can tell you firsthand the reason consignment is so challenging not only for a designer, but for the boutique owner as well. A friend of mine's niece wanted to open a new boutique, so they asked if I would meet with her to help out with any advice or suggestions. It turns out she wants to open a small, high-end boutique in a small resort town. She seemed pretty motivated and had a few years of experience working at another boutique. I offered to give her merchandise to fill her store, free of charge, and in return she would pay me when the product sold. This was not a total selfless act. The boutique she was opening was in a town I really wanted my clothing line to gain exposure in.

I worked diligently to have enough product to fill her racks. The first few weeks were a little unnerving as friends told me they stopped by the boutique, but it was never open. I called the owner and asked when she would begin holding regular hours, and she would respond, "It's not quite tourist season yet," or "The weather was terrible last weekend, I didn't think anybody would be out shopping." The fact of the matter is that this town is located on the water so rain dates are when most of the visitors go shopping, and the sunny days are when they are out boating.

The summer went on and I did sell some clothing, but I noticed a trend. The items in her store that she had purchased ended up displayed on a mannequin or showcased on a rack outside the store, whereas my items remained on the same two racks that were high on the wall and very difficult to reach. I called her each Monday to see how the weekly sales were. Was there anything particular her clients are looking for or anything that had sold that she would like me to bring more of? The answers became more and more vague: "Things are slow, but I'm sure they will pick up" was a common answer.

Let me put this into perspective, this resort town draws in people from Chicago and Grand Rapids and is one of the most-happening spots from May through August. Every day, from 10 a.m. on, you can hardly find a parking spot because there are so many visitors, not to mention the tourist buses. Her boutique, although very small, was located in the middle of the main drag, a great location. If she's not selling anything, either I have given her the wrong product or something else was wrong. So I commissioned a few friends to help me out. I asked them to stop by the boutique once a day to let me know what they saw. As it turned out, the boutique rarely held regular hours, and on top of that, she usually did not open until noon or later. Another disturbing discovery was the lack of customer service. I was informed that when my friends entered the boutique, whoever was working would sit at her desk with her head hidden behind a computer screen. She would glance up and say hello, but not another word. Nothing about the hand-dyed fabrics or that the store features a local designer—nothing. Again, my apparel would be on the higher racks that not one of my friends could reach; in fact one said she stood there on her tippy toes reaching and reaching, just trying to get the girl up from her computer desk to help her take down my clothes, without success. It turns out that it was not just my clothes that were not selling—nothing was selling because of the lack of service and crazy hours.

As the summer drew to an end, she began to have markdown sales in her store. Now, we had agreed on a fifty-fifty commission basis for my inventory. I chose this commission, because if she had purchased my apparel wholesale she would be doubling the price. So what happens when my merchandise goes on sale? This became very complicated. To top it off, I showed up at the store to find ten-dollar dresses hanging on an outside rack along with some other very poorly made, inexpensive apparel. Glancing at the tag on the inside I politely asked, "I've never heard of this brand, where did you find this designer?" She explained that she wanted to cater to high school students who cannot afford the higher-end apparel, so she found a website where she could bid on a large quantity of wholesale items. Not exactly the product I would envision my clothing hanging next to, but then again I did not have to worry about my clothes hanging next to these wholesale items since my apparel was still on the upper two racks that nobody could reach.

Needless to say, that was the last straw for me and I informed her I would be pulling my merchandise out the following week. I purposely left my clothing longer than most would because I was in the process of writing this book and I knew this would be an interesting story to share. I was able to see firsthand that when a boutique owner does not have some form of investment in your clothing, there is absolutely no incentive to push your items before the other brands they do have financial ties to. The other valuable lesson was just confirming what I have said about researching boutiques—be sure to find the perfect match for your apparel. Even if this owner had purchased my clothing wholesale to sell in her store, the lack of customer service and inconsistent hours turned off many of the would-be shoppers.

is late you will have to discount the price. Then you have *chargebacks,* which are discounts the larger retailer takes from you if your merchandise is ultimately sold to the consumer at a discount. If you are not abreast on the retailer's chargeback policies, adhering to them can really put a blow to your overall profit margin. So, if you sell your product to the retailer but your product does not sell as well or as fast as they expected and your merchandise goes on sale, they expect you to cover their loss. This was eye-opening for me, so make sure you know all the rules before you jump in. Another resource is one of the Fashion Business Incorporated seminars, EDI BootCamp (www.fashionbizinc.org). Usually an all-day seminar, they now offer this online. When you are ready to sell to the big retailers, make sure you understand all the rules.

Trade Shows

As your business grows, trade shows are an excellent way to expand your brand. Depending on which show you attend, you need to make sure you have the capabilities of manufacturing the quantities being ordered. The cost of attending a trade show can be quite high; have everything ready to present yourself and your collection in the best way possible. You need to grow thick skin. Buyers will make comments, and the experience can be harsh, but take all of the comments and feedback into consideration and learn from them.

Even if participating in a trade show is out of the question right now, you should try to visit a trade show as a spectator. Take note of how others have their booths set up; take in the entire experience so you can get an idea how the process works.

Trade Show Calendar

There are numerous trade shows to choose from, and each trade show caters to a different buyer or clientele. Visit WeConnectFashion.com for a calendar of events. This website has a wealth of information for fashion designers, including a calendar of all the trade shows with links to that particular show so you can easily research the event and apply to enter.

One of a Kind Show in Chicago

I recently visited a trade show in Chicago called One of a Kind, and I was amazed to see over six hundred artists showcasing their handmade work. The exhibits included all forms of art from clothing and jewelry to sculptures and paintings. There is an application process to apply for a booth; eligible work ranges from giftable craft to premium fine art. Artists will be juried and chosen based on uniqueness, craftsmanship, and attention to detail. The show is definitely first-class, offering fashion shows throughout the event to advertise different designer's collections, not to mention excellent PR throughout the year building up to the event. The show is held in the beginning of December, just in time for Christmas shopping. If you are designing higher-end or unique clothing, this show is a great opportunity to meet potential clients one-on-one and showcase your expertise.

The booth space is ten by ten feet, and there is storage room for excess inventory. Before you apply make sure you are capable of having enough inventory on hand. You can visit their website for additional information: oneofakindshowchicago.com.

Are You Ready for a Trade Show?

Regardless whether you have ten garments in your collection or fifty garments in your collection, you need to make sure you have the capability to manufacture your product before you take any orders from the trade show. If you leave the show with a ton of orders that you cannot fulfill, you will damage your reputation and will probably have a hard time selling in the future. I am not inferring that you need to sit and sew all of your orders, but you do need to have contractors lined up, along with funding to purchase your fabric and pay the contractors. Even if you have required a small deposit, you will not be paid in full from these stores until you deliver the items.

Cost

The cost involved in a trade show is more than just the price of a booth; there are other, extra items you need to take into consideration. If you attend three trade shows a year, you can figure on average $20,000 in expenses, but keep in mind these business expenses are tax deductible:

- Furniture
- Equipment
- Shipping
- Travel and hotel/lodging
- Entertainment
- Supplies
- Catalog
- Booth fee

Booth Space

If you already know which trade shows you plan on attending, sign your contract early because booth assignments are often first come, first served. Display your booth like a store, taking care not to over-merchandise. Have your samples on hand along with marketing materials. Make sure your booth space is neat and clean and well-organized. Make sure you are wearing your clothing, and possibly display some mannequins or posters from your last photo shoot.

Greet everyone that enters your booth. Introduce yourself and give a quick sales pitch. Buyers are cautious of first-timers, so if this is your first trade show it may take two or three times before they order from you. If you are already in some stores, be sure to mention the stores to the buyer. It is also a good idea to have someone work with you in the booth; this way if you need to take a break or grab lunch, someone is always available in your booth.

Combining with Other Designers

Lately, I have noticed a few opportunities for new designers to collaborate together in a booth for trade shows like StyleMax in Chicago and Magic in Las Vegas. Contact the Apparel Industry Board Inc. (AIBI) and Fashion Business Incorporated (FBI) for more information, and be sure to sign up for their mailing lists.

Hiring a Sales Rep

Once your clothing line begins to grow and you are keeping up with demand, you might consider hiring a sales rep. Sales reps usually represent a number of designers at the same time within a certain geographical area. Sales reps might attend trade shows, have connections with buyers at select department stores, and/or handle your samples in their showroom. Before even thinking of hiring a sales rep, however, make sure you have the means to fulfill any and all orders that you may receive. These are some things to think about when considering whether you should hire a sales rep:

- **Will a sales rep take your line?** As a new designer, you might have a hard time getting a sales rep to carry your line. As with anything else, it takes time to prove yourself as a designer and show that your clothing will sell. At the same time, not all sales reps are the right match to represent your line. Do your research and make sure you are choosing a reputable sale rep.

- **Compare what lines the rep is currently selling.** Not every sales rep is a perfect fit to represent your line. It is important to ask questions. What other lines does the sales rep currently represent? Are the other lines comparable to your collection in price point and style? Does the rep have connections to the stores buyers that you want to get into?
- **Understand the contract and payment terms.** When signing a contract with a sales rep make sure you check the length of time you are under contract. A sales rep usually works on a commission basis. You are responsible for paying this commission, but only after you are paid by the retail store. It would be a shame to pay your sales rep commission on a million-dollar order, only to have the store back out of their purchase.

Sales Strategy

With all the choices of how and where to sell your line, it is a good idea to pick out the sales strategy that will work with your business. Consider setting up a sales plan for the next three years; once your business gets started, you will be amazed how quickly time flies. For example, immediately open an online shop on BigCommerce.com and list your items. List any items that do not sell by the end of the season on eBay at a discount. Lay out plans for a fashion show once a year as a way to draw in new clients and cater to your existing clientele. In six months, prepare for a photo shoot with your new collection. From this photo shoot you can create a look book to send to boutiques and add new photos to your online store. In the meantime, research boutiques and set a goal of how many you plan on sending your look book to. Then plan ahead for a trade show; keep track of application deadlines and keep funds available. The more detailed your plans are, the better. Lay out the calendar with specific jobs to fill each week and make sure you stick to the schedule. It is really easy to get comfortable with a day-to-day schedule and forget about the future goals. Consider this calendar to be your boss and your link to greater sales and success.

It is funny how we spend so much time in school and then we are finished. Does that mean we are finished learning? I don't know about you, but the day I graduated from college I was so excited to begin buying books and learning about what I really wanted to do—fashion design! Still to this day I spend many a hours a week reading and learning about new things that I can adapt to my business: new technology for business, social media marketing strategies, new fabrics hitting the market, just to name a few. Can you imagine going to a doctor that never studied medicine after med school? Yikes! Every day there is new information for a fashion designer, including trend reports, new fabrication, sewing techniques that can save time and money, sales strategies, buying habits of consumers, and so much more. Of course we don't have a lot of extra time, but it is important to make the time to learn and stay ahead of your competitors. Never stop learning!

No matter what career path you take in life, you should always stay abreast of not only what is new in your industry, but continue to polish up on what you already know. In the business world this is called *continuing education*. When you work for yourself, there are a lot of responsibilities just keeping your day-to-day work load intact, especially when you are building your business. Yet it is still important to find the time to scan the fashion magazines for trends, shop the stores to see what is selling and what people are wearing, keep an eye on what is new in the technology world, and continue to expand and perfect your sewing and fitting skills.

Never Stop Learning

At least once a month I participate in online seminars or classes related to business, sewing, or fashion design. One new idea or business solution can make a huge difference in your business and keep you ahead of your competitors. Not to mention this is an easy way to try to stay abreast of the ever-changing technology and social media markets.

Online Classes

Fashion Business Incorporated (fashionbizinc.org) is one of my favorite websites to monitor for online classes strictly catered to the fashion designer, and you do not need to be a formal member in order to take their classes. Go to their website and join their e-mail list; this way you will be notified in advance of all of their upcoming classes and events. This website was started by Francis Harder, author of *Fashion for Profit,* another book you should put on your must-have list. The Apparel Industry Board Inc. also offers seminars and personal mentoring if you live in the Chicago area.

The Fashion Institute of Technology, Parsons, and other colleges that specialize in fashion have numerous quality classes, seminars, fashion shows, exhibits, and more. You do not have to sign up for a full load of classes either. If you are interested in attending college classes, check what is available online or evening classes if you do not want to interrupt your daily work schedule.

Free Seminars and Online Classes

Continuously monitor these sites for free seminar and online classes:

- FashionBizInc.org
- Pantone.com
- LinkedIn.com (various groups)

Seminars

All three of the websites listed below offer a complimentary magazine and free seminars with insights into the apparel and retail industries. Although not all of the information will be applicable to your needs, they offer great business information. Go to each website and sign up for their newsletter and magazine.

- RIS Retail Information Systems (www.risnews.edgl.com)
- CGT Consumer Goods Technology (www.consumergoods.edgl.com)
- Apparel (www.apparel.edgl.com)

Trade Shows

There are multiple fashion and textile trade shows all over the country. All you need is a business license and a business card to have access to the shows. Many of the shows offer insights into new fabrics and trend forecasting, and they're simply a way to show your face and network with other professionals.

Association of Sewing and Design Professionals (ASDP)

The Association of Sewing and Design Professionals (www.sewingprofessionals .org) has a mission to support individuals engaged in sewing and design related businesses, in both commercial and home-based settings including custom clothing, formal and bridal wear, design, pattern making, tailoring and alterations, accessories, costumes, wearable art, image consulting, production sewing, teaching and other industry-related avenues. The organization has over four hundred members nationwide and they hold an annual conference. The annual conference not only offers an opportunity to network with others in your field, there are multiple training classes to choose from in order to polish your skills in sewing, design, pattern making, and business.

Master Sewing and Design Professional Certification Program

The Master Sewing and Design Professional (MSDP) Certification Program is a performance-based program that was developed by the Association of Sewing and Design Professionals. It is based on ASDP's standards of quality and is open to anyone with a sewing-related business. MSDP certification provides the professional with the prestigious credentials that validate skills and expertise. The master certification will test your skills and knowledge in:

- Fabric
- Design
- Fashion illustration
- Fit
- Garment construction
- Pattern development
- Professional practices

For additional information e-mail certificateprogram@sewingprofessionals.org or visit the ASDP website (www.paccprofessionals.org).

Polish Your Sewing and Fitting Skills

If you are going to work in the alteration or custom apparel field, it is important that you continue to polish your sewing and fitting skills. Even if you strictly design a ready-to-wear line and never work with clients one-on-one, you might find some of these resources helpful when looking for inspiration for a collection. There are a few fitting books and videos available, including *The Complete Photo Guide to Perfect Fitting* by Sarah Veblen and *Threads* magazine's *Fitting* DVDs.

Expos

If you are looking for a three-day sewing retreat, just do an Internet search for the words "sewing expo" and you will be given a long list to choose from. At first glance, some of these might look a little bit too crafty or quilt oriented for a fashion designer, but in reality these places are filled with inspiration. The expos offer hands-on classes and seminars, many of which relate to apparel sewing, fit, and pattern altering. The vendor floor is filled with fabrics, notions, and embellishing ideas. Many times I will find new tools and techniques that I take home and add to my clothing designs. There are usually a handful of fashion shows featuring new patterns and ideas to inspire your creativity.

The American Sewing Expo (www.americansewingexpo.com) in Novi, Michigan, takes place the end of September and the Sewing and Stitchery Expo (www.sewingxxpo.com) in Puyallup, Washington, is held in the spring. Both of these have a reputation for attracting quality instructors and catering to the apparel sewer.

Books, Magazines, and Blogs

When I started my career as a custom clothier, I learned everything from books and magazines. My husband reminds me of the days when I dragged along my backpack filled with sewing books and fashion magazines (not to say *that* has changed much) every weekend we went boating. But the point is, I had passion, and I took the time to master the skills I needed to grow my business. I was able to teach myself couture sewing techniques, pattern drafting, draping, and fit, all from magazines and books, and you can do the same.

Amazon offers a unique book-buying experience. Every time you purchase a book related to fashion and sewing, Amazon will suggest twelve others that also relate to fashion and sewing. Just be sure to scan the reviews, because not all of the books carry quality information. Fashion-college libraries and bookstores are another place to look for information on the fashion design industry. I have included some of my favorite and highly recommended books in the appendix to get you started.

As far as sewing magazines, my two favorites that really focus on fashion, fitting, and sewing techniques would be *Threads* and *SewStylish*. Both magazines offer subscription rates or are available at your local fabric store. There is also an online archive of every issue of *Threads* magazine since the magazine began. Talk about a wealth of sewing information! The other thing I like about *Threads* magazine is that each month they review a current fashion designer, usually on the couture end, and they take you behind the scenes into their atelier. If you focus on high-end apparel, you will thoroughly enjoy this sewing magazine and gain insight into some of the couture sewing techniques.

Blogs are another great way to learn different sewing techniques. All you have to do is an Internet search on the sewing topic or technique you are interested in learning; you will be given plenty of options for free research. On top of that, many of them, including my own blog (www.angelawolf.wordpress.com), offer video tutorials.

Online Sewing Classes

PatternReview.com offers many online classes each month at a minimal cost. The classes cover sewing, fit, and fabric and usually include PDF files along with video.

This is a very easy way to learn new techniques, and you can communicate with the instructor and other class members. Access the classes at sewing.patternreview.com.

Keeping an Eye on Fashion and Trends

If you are designing apparel, it is essential to keep an eye on upcoming fashion trends. This does not mean that you have to follow the crowd, but staying aware of upcoming color and fashion trends can be very beneficial. Pantone and Mudpie have groups on LinkedIn that are well worth joining. They both offer free forecasts and occasional webinars within this group.

- Pantone.com. Pantone is your resource for keeping an eye on upcoming color trends. Make a note to visit their website occasionally; they offer a lot of free information along with a pay-for-service color forecasting. I personally rely on their free e-mails, which you can sign up for at their website.
- mpdclick.com. Another popular trend forecasting service is Mudpie. They also offer a few free articles and an e-mail newsletter.
- Design-Options.com. This is a trend and color forecasting service with a free newsletter and blog.
- Stylesight.com. This forecasting company has a phenomenal blog.
- Style.com. One of the easiest ways to keep tabs on what is hot each season is to view the fashion shows on Style.com. The website also offers information on current trends, what people are wearing on the streets, and other fashion-related news. I find flipping through the fashion shows is another way to get inspired.
- WWD.com. WWD also has an online site you can join, and if you can only afford one publication, it has to be *Women's Wear Daily*. This daily newspaper offers insight into what is going on in the fashion and apparel industry. From trend forecasting to the price of cotton, this publication covers it all, including designers, retail owners, and the executives that run the big brands. If it is happening in the fashion world, you will see it in the paper. You can also scan WWD.com for information, although parts of the website are only available with a subscription. Just a tip, if you are taking college classes or are a member of AIBI and some other organizations, you can get a discount on your WWD subscription.

13 Growing Pains...
Should You Go Big?

Probably the hardest part of working for yourself is realizing that your business has grown to a point that you just cannot do it all yourself. Just around my fifth year in business, my entire business was custom apparel and alterations, and I was faced with the decision to expand or not. I did everything myself from designing to sewing to everyday office work. I came to realize that if this did not change, I would never be able to expand or move forward past the point where I was at that moment. This was difficult for me to notice because I had spent the last five years so focused on everyday work that I did not take the time to look at the bigger picture. Something had to change; I was burning out from working twelve- to fifteen-hour days, and I was losing my vision and drive as an entrepreneur and fashion designer.

I consulted with my husband-to-be, my family, and a few other close mentors, and they all unanimously said the same thing: "Raise your prices! You are a classic example of supply and demand." I must admit, economics was my least favorite class in college, but I do recall the graphs of supply and demand. I just never related that to myself. My first reaction was that I would lose clients if I raised my prices; their response was that I might lose a few clients, but in the long run I would gain more.

This was very difficult for me. Many of my clients had been with me for years, and I hated the thought of potentially losing them. So instead of taking everyone's advice, I stayed the course. I continued to work ridiculous hours without improving my income or expanding my business. In fact, about one year later I found it difficult not only to sketch a new design but I dreaded going to the sewing room. I considered hiring someone, but I was not even sure where to start. In layman's terms, I was completely burnt out!

I toyed with the idea of working for someone else in the fashion industry or completely changing fields altogether. In order to keep busy and rationalize turning down custom jobs, I began to personal shop for some of my clients. Shopping for my clients at the higher-end stores opened my eyes to the reality of what my close friends had been telling me: People will pay the money for quality, which is what I was offering with my custom work. This is exactly why I mentioned earlier in the book to make sure you take the time and visit stores that are comparable to what you are selling. Not only will this build your confidence if you are offering a quality product but you will gain insight into what other brands are charging. So I spent the next two years reevaluating my business model, focusing strictly on personal shopping and doing alterations in order to keep tabs on fashion and continue a relationship with my clients.

Thinking of Expanding

Once I finally took the time to step back and really analyze my overall business, I could see that I had a major decision to make. Am I going to keep my business smaller and focus strictly on a select clientele with custom apparel or should I expand? Keep in mind, bigger is not always better. It is just fine keeping your business smaller; this really allows you to focus on your expertise. In fact, there are cases in many industries, not just fashion, that when a company expanded too quickly or did not have the right resources at hand to handle the expansion, they ended up going out of business. So when you get to the point of considering expansion, make sure you lay out your plan in detail and consider all of the additional costs involved—even how your position will change. Will you be spending more of your time training and managing employees? If so, who will do the work you previously were responsible for? What about the extra cost of moving to a larger facility? You currently are working out of your home, and although you incur some additional business costs there, it is nothing like renting another location where you will have an entire list of expenses added to what you will still be paying for your home: rent, utilities, Internet, phone, added gas for traveling to and from work, and security system, just to mention a few.

You might consider writing a new business plan. This will allow you to lay out all of your ideas and concepts for expansion and work out the kinks. It is amazing how differently things appear on paper than what you might be imagining in your head. Another thing that I did was list the pros and cons of moving my business out of my home. In all reality, I probably should have moved my business out of my house years beforehand, so my list of pros and cons was mostly pros.

Cons:

- Additional expense
- Cannot sew in the middle of the night

Pros:

- Separation of work and personal life
- Regular hours for clients
- No random visitors at our home
- All of the business will be in one location
- Larger space
- Easier to organize
- Do not have to shovel (included in my rent)
- Room for mannequins and a better layout
- Get my home back

Opening Your Own Studio

For me, the decision was very clear: Either move my studio to a new location or close my business. I know that sounds drastic, but my business had taken over my entire life and my entire house, and something needed to change. I was already moving to a new house, and I wanted a home not a shop, so this was the perfect time to move to a studio. My first studio was located on the fourth floor of a professional building. I did not have retail at that time, so there was no need to pay all the extra money for a street level location, something you might want to consider as well if you are trying to keep the costs down. A few other things to take into account when looking for a place: location of the building, an elevator for clients, security or doorman who takes packages for the building (that is a plus), and ease of access and parking. But there is one you might not have considered: sunlight. Direct sunlight can fade your fabric and garments in a very short time. If you have large windows, make sure they can be covered, or if you have an option, choose a studio that does not have direct sunlight in the morning and afternoon. Check a few locations before signing a lease, and if you are responsible for paying your own utilities, ask to see copies of previous bills. A friend of mine rented a large open space studio, and her first electric bill (during heating season) was over $1,000. Added with her rent of $1,500, it almost put her out of business. So make sure you know all your costs up front.

There are a few ways to save money when moving your business outside of your home. Instead of installing a new business phone line, consider forwarding the business line you have set up at home to your cell phone. To save from having to install new Internet, turn your cell phone or tablet into a hotspot. This will allow you to have Internet wherever you are, home or studio, with just one charge.

As you move all the equipment and supplies from your home to your new studio, take the extra effort to organize and lay out your space as you are moving. Think of it as spring cleaning. You might find items that you do not need any longer; if so, get rid of them. Organizing as you go will allow you to jump back into work quite quickly.

Hiring a Subcontractor

If you come to the realization that you cannot expand while continuing to do everything yourself, you will need to hire some help. For me the question became, where do I start? Do I hire someone to sew, cut, or help with office work? Which job can and should I pass on?

For this chapter I conferred with Janet Pray, president of the American Sewing Expo and owner of the Islander Sewing Systems. Janet experienced firsthand what it was like to be in a deadlock: To expand or not? Janet was creating and selling a ready-to-wear line, and it became obvious to her that she could not improve her income while continuing on all by herself. She decided to hire others to sew on a subcontract basis. With references from the local sewing guild, Janet began to look for other sewers who she could potentially hire to work from their own homes. She says the first step in finding qualified individuals was to interview the candidates over the phone. In the interview Janet would inquire as to their sewing ability and knowledge of basic sewing skills. If the potential seamstress passed the phone interview, she was then required to bring Janet two outfits in order to show her experience and quality standard. Janet insists the most important thing to look for is a high quality standard. Through time you can teach basic sewing skills, but quality standard is something you are not likely to change. If your potential seamstress brings you work that is sloppy, that is what you are going to get back, and your expectations should not be anything more.

Janet continued to do the cutting herself. As she puts it, "If someone cuts the garment off-grain, the garment is ruined from the beginning. If there is an error while sewing, that can usually be adjusted in order to salvage the garment." So Janet would give each seamstress a bundle that included the cut pattern, interfacing, notions, thread, and anything else needed to sew the entire garment from start to finish.

Since the seamstress would be taking the work home to sew, Janet wanted to make sure that there were no questions on how to accurately construct the garment. Each seamstress would come in and watch Janet sew the particular item from beginning to end. Janet would teach them production sewing using industrial sewing techniques, which are faster and more efficient than traditional home sewing techniques. Even if the new industrial sewing technique was foreign to the seamstress, she had them practice; usually by the third time they understood it. Janet also gave them a booklet to take home, outlining the basic steps, including dimensions and specifics, for example, a quarter-inch, double-turn hem at the bottom of the shirt.

Armed with some specific instructions, a sample garment, a bundle, and a booklet, each seamstress would work from the comfort of her own home on her own work schedule. Janet said she allowed each seamstress to set her own quota. Some of the workers had children at home and could only work in the evening hours, so they might only choose to make twelve garments a week. Others used this opportunity as their full-time job, and they might have taken home twenty-six or thirty bundles for the week. Janet made it very clear to the seamstress when they picked up their bundles what day these needed to be returned as finished garments. She would keep in constant contact with them on a weekly basis, and if someone was behind schedule or had a family emergency or something come up and they were unable to finish the garment, she would remind them not to wait until the last minute to call her. If they were unable to finish their job by the designated date, she needed to know so she could pass the work onto others.

Warning!

Take note: If you live in California or New York it is illegal to manufacture clothing from your own home.

Paying Your Workers

Be up front about when you are going to pay your subcontractors. Are you going to pay them when they drop off the finished garment? Once a month or weekly? However you plan on paying your workers, they need to know and agree upon your terms before you give them any work to take home. At the same time, never pay them until the work is finished.

When you are first starting out, cash flow will probably be tight. Janet recalls the times she was getting ready for a show in September and cash flow was very stressed from purchasing the supplies for her garments. She asked the seamstresses if they would be willing to work all of August, and she would pay them immediately after her show in September. All of the workers were fine with this agreement, but at least she gave them an option to say no.

Confirming a Subcontractor Agreement

Explain to your seamstress what it is to work as a subcontractor. First of all, they need to check their local township for any rules or laws that might prevent them from being able to work from their home. Next, they need to understand that annually (by February 28) you will give them an IRS Form 1099-MISC stating the amount of money you have paid them in a year, and in return they will need to pay taxes on this income. Janet said she would suggest to her subcontractors to automatically take

Hiring In versus Hiring Out

While interviewing Janet Pray, president of America Sewing Expo and Islander Sewing Systems, I asked her to give me a positive and a negative of hiring your own home-sewing subcontractor versus sending your work to a factory.

Positive:

It allows you to work on a piecemeal basis, especially if you are selling directly to the consumer or small boutiques. This gives you the ability to manufacture your clothing on a small scale, without a huge commitment.

Negative:

You have to micromanage everything, whereas if you sent your bundles to a factory, they would handle all of the daily issues.

25 percent to 30 percent of each check and put it into a savings account. This way at the end of the year when taxes came due, there would not be any surprises, and they would have the money to pay what was owed. Technically, your seamstresses are self-employed, and they should file for their own DBA. By applying for their own business license, they will then be able to take advantage of certain tax write-offs such as mileage, sewing machine repairs, and miscellaneous sewing supplies.

Hiring an Assistant

Maybe you are inclined to hire someone to just help with everyday errands and office paperwork. Even if you are hiring for a part-time job, you need to lay out exactly what is required of your new employee. List all of the jobs that he or she will be responsible for and the skills required for each job. This will help you to weed out the perfect employee along with having a standard to check their progress against every six months.

When hiring an employee, part-time or full-time, there are specific government filings and paperwork you need to have in order, as mentioned in chapter 7. Consult with your accountant so you have all of the correct information.

Interns

College interns are a great option when looking for assistance. Most of the time, the interns will work at no charge in exchange for the information and knowledge they will gain by working with you. Keep in mind, just because an intern is going to college for fashion design does not mean they are a qualified assistant for what you need. Interview an intern the same way you would interview a potential employee. If they are agreeing to work for you at no charge, you need to find out from them what they are expecting to learn from you. For example, if an intern wants to learn draping and pattern making and you have him or her entering receipts on the computer all day, this is not a fair trade.

Preventing Burnout

As your career continues, certain skills and talents of yours will begin to stand out. Focus on what you are good at and try to become the best in that area. It is better to be meticulous in one or two main areas than to be mediocre in a dozen areas. Staying focused and knowing exactly which clients you are trying to cater to will help to prevent you from wandering into areas that will not benefit your business.

Make sure you only commit yourself to what you know you can accomplish. Keep close tabs on the hours you schedule for work and try to maintain a balance between your personal life and your business. This is even more important if you have a husband and/or children. My husband's philosophy is "the perfect balance in life is to work eight hours, sleep eight hours, and play eight hours." Although I have never quite reached that perfect balance, it is something to think about and strive for.

Remember You Cannot Be Everything to Everyone!

As I mentioned earlier in the book, the most important motto that you should live by in any career, but especially in fashion, is to remember that you cannot be everything to everyone. If only I could have a dollar for every time I have received a request for something I do not offer: "I wish you made plus-size clothing," "I wish your jackets were not so tailored," or my favorite, "Your clothing is so young, what about us older ladies?" I used to get very defensive when somebody approached me with a statement like this, but later on I realized that this is a compliment to how focused my collections really are. I specialize in fit, quality, and tailoring—that is my signature. I also know that I am trying to cater to the younger, trendier client with an active lifestyle, although *age* is a broad term; I have sixty-year-old women purchasing the same designs as my thirty-year-old clients. I do not carry plus-size clothing, but I offer a custom option for an additional fee. The point is, stick to your niche. Keep this phrase in the back of your mind, especially when working with clients one-on-one. Know when to say no, and do not feel bad about it.

Are You a Seamstress or Are You a Fashion Designer?

When you are doing the designing and sewing yourself from your home, there will come a time when you are faced with a difficult question: Are you a seamstress or are you a fashion designer? Neither is bad; in fact both offer very viable income resources. If your main focus is to become a fashion designer, even if you have accepted other sewing jobs in order to build your skills and your reputation in your local area, you will eventually need to prioritize your workload. After I stepped away from my daily workload, I was able to see the mistakes I had made. My main goal from day one was to design a line of women's high-end apparel. Without realizing it, I had allowed my alteration business to take over every hour of every day. There are only so many hours in the day, so when you are the main talent in your business, use those hours wisely.

Stick to What You Are Good At

If I look back at the times that I ended up with a disaster on my hands, it was almost always when I said yes to a client when I knew I should have said no. There is something to be said about having a gut instinct, and do not be afraid to follow it. There is something to be said about having a "main focus" and not swaying too far from it.

No matter how badly you want the business, especially when you are first starting out, if someone asks you to design or sew something that is out of your realm, save yourself the headache and hours of frustration by simply saying no. Through time, you will gain respect and acknowledgment for the talents that you do have.

Getting Focused

Every six months, take time to analyze how your business has grown or changed. Are you focusing your time and energy where it needs to be in order for your business to grow and expand the way that you envision? List any of the daily tasks that need to change in order to keep you more focused. If you are designing a collection, are you maintaining consistency with your design aesthetic season after season? If you have veered or gotten sidetracked, map out a game plan to get back on track. Was your goal to have your collection sold in four boutiques by this time and you realize you have spent the last six months with your head under a sewing machine doing alterations? Refocus your attention where it needs to be, and your business will grow faster than you could ever imagine.

When I started my fashion design business, I was in the dark on many aspects, but through trial and error I continued on. I hope the experiences I shared in this book will help you to bypass a few of the pitfalls, but do not get discouraged if you are faced with new challenges. Take each struggle as a learning lesson that will make you smarter and stronger in the future.

Try to take the time to join a few of the groups mentioned for networking, especially in the fashion and sewing industries. Many of the friends I've made through the Association of Sewing and Design Professionals I have never met in person, but I can always learn and get a laugh from a few of them on ASDP's private discussion list. At the same time, feel free to drop me a note at any time; I would love to hear how your new fashion design career is taking off. That's it! Go get started and remind yourself every day to stop for a moment, smell the roses, and thank God for your talents. Good luck!

Business and Fashion Organizations to Join

The Apparel Industry Board Inc.
www.aibi.com

Association of Sewing and Design Professionals
www.paccprofessionals.org

Business Networking International
www.bni.com

Council of Fashion Designers of America
www.cfda.com

Fashion Business Incorporated
www.fashionbizinc.org

Fashion Group International Inc.
www.fgi.org

GenArt
www.genart.org

National Sewing Council
www.nationalsewingcouncil.org

Rotary International
www.rotary.org

Business of Fashion

Books

Arrington, Jay, and Michael H. *How to Effectively Sell Your Clothing Line to Retailers*. Harper Arrington Publishing, 2004.

———. *The Reality of Owning and Operating Your Own Clothing Line*. Harper Arrington Publishing, 2004.

Calderin, Jay. *Form, Fit, and Fashion: All the Details Fashion Designers Need to Know but Can Never Find*. Rockport Publishers, 2009.

Harder, Francis. *Fashion for Profit: From Design Concept to Manufacturing and Retailing; A Complete Professional's Guide,* 9th ed. Harder Publications, 2010.

Meadows, Toby. *How to Set up and Run a Fashion Label*. Laurence King Publishers, 2009.

Okonkwo, Uche. *Luxury Fashion Branding: Trends, Tactics, Techniques.* Palgrave Macmillan, 2007.

Websites

www.apparel.edgl.com

www.apparelnews.net

www.balluun.com

www.consumergoods.edgl.com

www.copyright.gov/eco

www.ftc.gov

www.oneofakindshowchicago.com

www.risnews.edgl.com

www.startingaclothingline.com

www.weconnectfashion.com

Credit Card Merchants

www.intuit.com

www.intuit-gopayment.com

www.paypal.com

www.samsclub.com

www.squareup.com

Educational Material for Sewing and Design

Books

Burns, Leslie, and Nancy Bryant. *The Business of Fashion: Designing, Manufacturing, and Marketing*. Fairchild Publications, 2007.

Fasanella, Kathleen. *The Entrepreneur's Guide to Sewn Product Manufacturing.* Apparel Technical Services, 1998.

Gehlhar, Mary. *The Fashion Designer Survival Guide*. Kaplan Publishing, 2008.

Khalje, Susan. *Bridal Couture: Fine Sewing Techniques for Bridal Wear and Evening Gowns.* Krause Publications, 1997.

Klaman, Stacey L., Karen Kunkel, and Barbara Fimbel. *The Experts Book of Sewing Tips and Techniques: From the Sewing Stars; Hundreds of Ways to Sew Better, Faster, Easier.* Rodale Press, 1995.

Meadows, Toby. *How to Set Up and Run a Fashion Label.* Laurence King Publishing Ltd., 2009.

Shaeffer, Claire B. *Claire Shaeffer's Fabric Sewing Guide,* 2nd ed. Krause Publications, 2008.

———. *High Fashion Sewing Secrets from the World's Best Designers: A Step-By-Step Guide to Sewing Stylish Seams, Buttonholes, Pockets, Collars, Hems, And More.* Rodale Books, 2001.

Vogue Knitting Magazine. Vogue Sewing, Revised and Updated. Sixth & Spring Books, 2006.

Magazines and Television

It's Sew Easy PBS series
www.itsseweasytv.com

SewStylish Magazine

Threads Magazine
www.threadsmagazine.com
Training DVDs also available

Websites

www.americansewingexpo.com
www.brookscollege.edu
www.fashion-enter.com
www.fitnyc.edu
www.governmentgrants.org
www.islandersewing.com
www.parsons.edu
www.patternreview.com
www.score.org
www.sewingexpo.com
www.whorepresents.com

Fabric and Other Sewing Resources

www.aboutsources.com

www.banaschs.com

www.bandjfabrics.com

www.charmwoven.com

www.clothinglabels4u.com

www.dill-buttons.com

www.elliottbermantextiles.com

www.fabricmartfabrics.com

www.fashiondex.com

www. fishmansfabrics.com

www.ftwfabric.com

www.gorgeousfabrics.com

www.habermanfabrics.com

www.jbsilks.com

www.kaiscissors.com

www.moodfabrics.com

www.paulanadelstern.com

www.richlinfabrics.com

www.sewtrue.com

www.supremefabrics.com

www.voguefabricsstore.com

www.wawak.com

www.xpresalabels.com

Fashion Sketching

Books

Burke, Sandra. *Fashion Artist: Drawing Techniques to Portfolio Presentation, 2nd ed.* Burke Publishing, 2006.

Ireland, Patrick John. *New Fashion Figure Templates.* B. T. Batsford, 2007.

Travers-Spencer, Simon, and Zarida Zaman. *The Fashion Designer's Directory of Shape and Style.* Barron's Educational Series, 2008.

Websites

www.carolkimball.nct
www.designersnexus.com
www.howtodrawfashion.com
www.mypracticalskills.com

Fashion and Trends

Magazines
GAP PRESS
Runway Magazine
Women's Wear Daily

Websites

www.apparelnews.net
www.cadenamujer.com
www.design-options.com
www.mpdclick.com
www.pantone.com
www.style.com
www.stylesight.com
http://trendjournal.mudpie.co.uk

Pattern Making, Fitting, and Draping

Books

Amaden-Crawford, Connie. *The Art of Fashion Draping,* 4th ed. Fairchild Publishing, 2012.

———. *Grading Workbook.* Amaden-Crawford, 2011.

———. *Patternmaking Made Easy,* 2nd ed. Amaden-Crawford, 2007.

Fashiondex Inc., editor. *The Apparel Design and Production Hand Book: A Technical Reference.* Fashiondex, 2001.

Hollen, Norma, and Carolyn Kundel. *Pattern Making by the Flat-Pattern,* 7th ed. Prentice-Hall, 1993.

Joseph-Armstrong, Helen. *Draping for Apparel Design,* 2nd ed. Fairchild Publications, 2008.

———. *Patternmaking for Fashion Design,* 5th ed. Prentice Hall, 2009.

Price, Jeanne, and Bernard Zamkoff. *Grading Techniques for Fashion Design,* 2nd ed. Fairchild Publications, 1996.

Stringer, Pamela. *Pattern Drafting for Dressmaking.* B. T. Batsford, 1992.

Veblen, Sarah. *The Complete Photo Guide to Perfect Fitting.* Creative Publishing International, 2012.

Websites

www.dressriteforms.com

www.fashionpatterns.com

www.pgmdressforms.com

www.wolfform.com

www.zipppershop.com

Pattern-Making Software

www.gerbertechnology.com

www.optitex.com

www.patternmakerusa.com

Sewing and Alterations

Books

Roehr, Mary A. *Altering Women's Ready-to-Wear.* Mary Roehr Custom Tailoring, 1987.

Weiland, Barbara. *Secrets for Successful Sewing.* Rodale Books, 2000.

Wright Sykes, Barbara. *Pricing without Fear.* Collins Publications, 2005.

Websites

www.jsmtailoringtools.com

www.lindastewartcouturedesigns.com

Styling and Wardrobe Planning

Books

Allen, Jeanne. *Dressing with Color: The Designer's Guide to Over 1,000 Color Combinations.* Chronicle Books, 1992.

Bryant, Janie, and Monica Harel. *The Fashion File: Advice, Tips, and Inspiration from the Costume Designer of Mad Men.* Grand Central Life & Style, 2010.

Editors of InStyle Magazine. *The New Secrets of Style: Your Complete Guide to Dressing Your Best Every Day.* InStyle, 2009.

Garza, Jesse, and Joe Lupo. *Work It! A Guide to Your Ultimate Career Wardrobe.* Chronicle Books, 2009.

Klensch, Elsa. *Style.* Berkley Publishing Group, 1995.

Mason Mathis, Carla, and Helen Villa Conner. *The Triumph of Individual Style.* Fairchild Publications, 2002.

Nix-Rice, Nancy. *Looking Good: Wardrobe Planning and Personal Style Development.* Palmer/Pletsch Publishing, 1996.

Rasband, Judith. *Wardrobe Strategies for Women.* Fairchild Publications, 1996.

Websites

www.fashionforrealwomen.com/blog/

www.nancynixrice.com

www.wardrobeconsulting.blogspot.com

Website Design and Selling Online

www.advanquest.com

www.bigcommerce.com

www.ebay.com

www.etsy.com

www.godaddy.com

www.intuit.com

www.serif.com/webplus

www.shopify.com

www.shoppista.com

www.wix.com

www.wordpress.com

Index

Italicized page numbers indicate photographs.

About the Author

Angela Wolf is the owner of ABO Apparel, LLC, and an internationally renowned fashion designer, TV personality, speaker, instructor, and author. Angela graduated with a business degree from Illinois State University. With a new sewing machine and serger as a graduation gift from family, she started a home-based custom apparel business. With the encouragement of her (now) husband, she created an eighteen-piece collection and held a private fashion show for local women. This show launched Angela's career in custom couture in 1994, and in 2010 she launched her first ready-to-wear (RTW) collection.

Winner of the 2008 Passion for Fashion award, in 2010 Angela was one of the featured fashion designers participating in Chicago Showcase Fashion Event put on by the Apparel Industry Board and chaired by Mayor Richard Daley. Angela is also the couture-sewing expert on the PBS series *It's Sew Easy*. With added exposure in the sewing industry, Angela has launched a pattern collection for the home sewer. Each season she offers patterns to coincide with her RTW collection. You can find the patterns at AngelaWolfPatterns.com.

Angela writes a monthly "Fashion and Trends" column on PatternReview .com and is a frequent contributor to *Threads* and *SewStylish* magazines. With a passion for designing quality clothing and exploring her love for creating new trends and techniques, Angela continues to share her talent by teaching and speaking all over the country.